Unlocking the Ancient Secret . . .

"Robert's new book beckons you into a place of intimacy and true relationship. You will be revitalized and refreshed in your spirit to seek what is acceptable in living lifestyles of worship unto the Lord."

Mike Bickle
DIRECTOR, INTERNATIONAL HOUSE OF PRAYER OF KANSAS CITY

"Robert is a passionate Levite with courageous faith and passion for God. His writing is accomplished and we know that he has the character and lifestyle to back up his words. This book will bring you to the ultimate place of laying down your life as an authentic worshipper. Let yourself be impacted by the heart of a worshipping warrior."

Wesley and **Stacey Campbell**
FOUNDERS, PRAYING THE BIBLE INTERNATIONAL

"We have so appreciated the heart of prayer and worship that Robert Stearns has modeled. Founded on a focus of prayer for Israel, America, and the nations, Robert leads us into practical steps so that we may develop a lifestyle of worship. Every believer looking for the appearing of our Lord needs to prepare his bridal heart with worship. This is a handbook for the bride to prepare for the Bridegroom's coming."

Mahesh and **Bonnie Chavda**
SENIOR PASTORS, ALL NATIONS CHURCH

"God is a consuming fire and the flames of His awesome presence are heading your way! This book will take you deeper than you've ever been in a true understanding of acceptable worship. Get ready to catch fire!"

Dr. Dick Eastman
INTERNATIONAL PRESIDENT, EVERY HOME FOR CHRIST

"Robert Stearns is one of the clearest voices sounding the prophetic counsel of God today. In his book *Keepers of the Flame*, he calls us to a lifestyle of worship that goes beyond experience and into a face-to-face relationship with Jesus. The message contained in these pages is one that has been seasoned through the years in Robert's personal life. That is why it rings with such authenticity and authority. The moral and cultural landscape of America has dramatically changed—and the Church has all too often been shaped by the culture rather than penetrating and shaping culture. That is why the Church needs to hear this message. If ever there was a time that we needed to understand how we as a Church are to be the sweet smelling aroma or worship to the Lord—it is now!"

Steve Fry
Senior Pastor, Belmont Church, Nashville, TN

"With penetrating insight, *Keepers of the Flame*, catapults the reader into a higher vision of what true intercession and worship is about. With the voice of a pioneer, Robert Stearns urges you to go into the fire of God's presence and be transformed into a vessel which knows God's ways and obtains character to carry the fire. A timely and needed word!"

James W. Goll
Cofounder of Ministry to the Nations

"In a day when Christians are being easily distracted, Robert Stearns calls us back to the simplicity of loving God. This book inspired me to keep the flame of worship burning in my heart at all times."

J. Lee Grady
Editor, Charisma

"Does your heart resonate with a yearning to know God more? Since knowing God passionately is a life-long journey, this book will move you closer to knowing God deeper. Robert Stearns is not only a dear friend but also my covenant brother, who has touched my life very deeply. Every one of us possesses a hunger to know God in a deeper way. *Keepers of the Flame* is a life-changing message for every believer who is hungry to know God more. This book will challenge you in your concept of worship and will expand your outlook making you step beyond your experience of Sunday morning worship. This message has been burning in Robert's heart for past three years and is a *kairos* truth for us right now. This life-changing invitation from his heart will remind you, the elements of worship can never replace the essence of worship. Are you ready for this adventure into a life of true worship?"

Sam Hinn
Senior Pastor, The Gathering Place Worship Center

"In every generation, God raises up a David—someone who passionately ushers in the presence of God through worship. Robert Stearns is a "David" in our day, as evidenced through his insight offered in *Keepers of the Flame*. This timely book captures the essence of the timeless truths God gave to His ancient Israel."

David D. Ireland, Ph.D.
AUTHOR AND SENIOR PASTOR, CHRIST CHURCH, MONTCLAIR, NJ

"Keepers of the Flame sheds new light and brings understanding from the shadows of the old to the reality of the new. The relationship between the altar, sacrifice, and fire is truly a type of the Body of Christ in its steps towards united worship. The sweet smelling fragrance of worship that God searches for is more than personal; it is a united, corporate expression which includes the three aspects laid out so clearly in this relevant text. A must for individual or group study."

Rev. Paul Johansson
PRESIDENT, ELIM BIBLE INSTITUTE, LIMA, NY

"Keepers of the Flame is a clear prophetic message to the church of our generation. The Holy Spirit uses Robert to compel us to become authentic worshippers as we make the presence of a holy God the number one priority in our daily lives. Then we can receive grace to experience genuine relationships. I highly recommend this book!"

Larry Kreider
INTERNATIONAL DIRECTOR, DOVE CHRISTIAN FELLOWSHIP INTERNATIONAL

"Without a doubt, Robert Stearns has a very fervent heart. He loves God and is passionate about his walk with God. That passion definitely comes out in this book, *Keepers of the Flame*. The reader is led through a variety of challenges from private to public life where the fire of God must burn. At the close, the invitation to make a commitment takes these truths and walks them right into the reader's life."

Don Meyer, Ph.D.
PRESIDENT, VALLEY FORGE CHRISTIAN COLLEGE

"Robert Stearns' new book is sure to inspire readers to move into the Biblical design for worship. His understanding of the romance of the Gospel calls us to new passion and intimacy with God. This book will rock you out of your comfort zone and make you examine your heart as a worshipper and warrior. The renewal and intimacy pathway that Stearns traces through the Bible will ignite your passion for all that God has for you."

Rev. Dr. David M. Midwood
PRESIDENT, VISION NEW ENGLAND

"Robert Stearns with his years of experience in the area of praise and worship has captured one of the most crucial revelations of intimacy with God in worship and provides practical and insightful principles to keep the presence of God in your daily life. This is a must-read for the heart desperate for God's presence."

Dr. Myles Munroe
BAHAMAS FAITH MINISTRIES INTERNATIONAL, NASSAU, BAHAMAS

"Robert Stearns has written a thoughtful and provoking book on the centrality of worship in our lives and churches. Many of Robert's observations are arresting and invite us into serious self-examination. The convictions behind this book provide crucial direction for those who would seek God with all their hearts, soul, mind, and strength."

Dr. Mac Pier
PRESIDENT, CONCERTS OF PRAYER GREATER NEW YORK

"This is a time in history that the Ancient of Days is beginning to release wisdom that has been reserved for *this age* (1 Cor. 2:7). The fear of the Lord is the beginning of wisdom. As we worship, we begin to know Him and become a living, walking sacrifice in the earth realm. *This* is more than a book about worship. This book represents communion, sacrifice, passion and fire. We are called to endure in the race of life until we meet our Heavenly Father face to face. *Keepers of the Flame* lights your fire so you can run the race with supernatural, abundant grace and joy which releases overcoming strength!"

Chuck Pierce
VICE PRESIDENT, GLOBAL HARVEST MINISTRIES
PRESIDENT, GLORY OF ZION INTERNATIONAL

"Keeping the flame of God fueled and fanned is a calling that Robert Stearns has personally heard and obeyed. Through his anointed worship leading many thousands have been richly blessed. Now through *Keepers of the Flame*, even more multitudes of the body of Christ will be blessed and challenged to ensure that all aspects of our lives are *acceptable* sacrifices to God. Robert's haunting question, "Is God hearing us?", raises the possibility that though today's Church may have all the accoutrements of worship, perhaps the wood on the altar is wet, soaked in the self-absorption that is so much a part of our culture. This book is a *shofar* call to take seriously our priestly responsibility of the altar, the acceptable sacrifice we offer to God, and the fire."

Dr. David Schroeder
PRESIDENT, NYACK COLLEGE & ALLIANCE THEOLOGICAL SEMINARY

"God is so worthy of our worship, 11-12 on Sunday morning is just not enough! The Old Testament Levites worshiped 24-7 with a profound sense of awe and focus. Today, God is raising up a new generation of Levites in the earth who will walk in daily worship to invite a divine habitation. *Keepers of the Flame* is a rally call for this new Order of Levites that will help us move beyond being mere consumers to being consumed by the His Presence. This book would have been required reading in The Temple book store."

Terry Teykl
PRAYER-EVANGELIST WITH RENEWAL MINISTRIES, HOUSTON, TEXAS

KEEPERS
of the FLAME

ABOUT THE AUTHOR

Robert Stearns is the Founder and Executive Director of Eagles' Wings, a dynamic, relational ministry community involved in a variety of outreaches and strategic projects around the world. Robert's ministry flows out of deep passion for Jesus that is characterized by a distinct prophetic edge. He and the Eagles' Wings team are dedicated to bringing unity and awakening to the global Body of Christ, and maintain offices in the US and Europe. He has ministered in 30 nations around the world and maintains a significant burden for the Eastern United States and for Israel.

Robert has ministered extensively throughout North America, Israel, Europe, Australia, and Central America. In Israel, he has been a guest artist and worship leader at several celebrations of the Feast of Tabernacles, and has ministered in conferences and gatherings throughout the land. Robert has sung before three Prime Ministers of Israel, including a special concert for former Prime Minister Benjamin Netanyahu. He served as the Executive Director of "The Call New York City", which gathered 80,000 people for prayer and fasting in New York City in June 2002. He is the founder and visionary behind the *Lord, Teach Us to Pray* worship and intercession training seminars, which have made a significant impact on churches throughout the Greater New York City area. Robert is a member of the National Mission America Coalition Committee.

A powerful communicator, Robert has been a featured guest columnist in both *Charisma* and *Ministries Today* magazines, and is in demand internationally as a keynote speaker. He is an author, having published *Prepare the Way* and this book, *Keepers of the Flame*. Robert is an accomplished recording artist, worship leader and soloist with 7 CD's having been released in the past several years. He has appeared on television on the *700 Club* with Pat Robertson, *100 Huntley St.*, and *Praise the Lord* on the Trinity Broadcasting Network, and on numerous other television and radio programs.

Robert serves on the Board of Advisors for *Ministries Today* magazine; he is Publisher of *KAIROS* magazine; Executive Producer of the *House of David* radio broadcast, as well as Executive Director of the Israel Experience College Scholarship Program.

Robert, his wife Ana, and their son Isaac, live in New York and spend a great deal of time in Jerusalem, Israel.

KEEPERS
of the FLAME

Unlocking the Ancient Secret of an Acceptable Sacrifice

ROBERT STEARNS

K | KAIROS PUBLISHING®

Keepers of the Flame
Copyright © 2003 by Robert Stearns

Published by Kairos Publishing
PO Box 450
Clarence, NY 14031
www.kairos.us

Library of Congress Catalog Number: 2003-113212
ISBN: 0-9665831-4-0

Cover Design: Peter Ecenroad
Interior Design: David G. Danglis / Pinwheel Creative
Editors: Larry Keefauver and Sarah Wolf

CONTENTS

DEDICATION

This book is dedicated to the Jewish people, who throughout history, against all odds, and often at the greatest personal cost, have carried the testimony of the One True God in the earth. They have been *keepers of the flame.*

And, to Rabbi Dr. Gerald Meister and David Nekrutman, who embody those values; for their courage and commitment to the God of Israel.

ACKNOWLEDGEMENTS

Writing this book has certainly been a collaborative process, and I am thankful to many people for their help, directly or indirectly, in seeing this project birthed.

First of all, I am thankful to my wife, Ana, who is the most amazing human being I know. She is a fountain of blessing for all who have the privilege of knowing her. Her love has added meaning and fulfillment to my life. And, in the middle of this project, she blessed me with the birth of our first born, a son named Isaac. May he live his life as a *keeper of the flame.*

My grandmother, Ronnie Rosar, continues to be an inspiration and strength. Eighty-four years young at the time of this writing, she has more vitality than most 20 year olds I know. She is a woman of deep faith and prayer, and her life has touched and been an example for so many. She is loved and respected by all, especially me!

The Eagles' Wings community has some of the finest, most dedicated, focused, humble people I have ever encountered. I am so thankful for our Leadership Team: Stephen Jenks, Sue Ten Eyck, and Jeff Reiff, for their love and support over many years. They do so much behind the scenes that makes a great difference in the Body of Christ and in my life personally.

The friends and family of Eagles' Wings, the Impact Destiny Team, are those who faithfully pray and support us in our efforts in God's Kingdom. We could not be released to do what we do without you. This book is a product of your faithful partnership in the Gospel.

Dr. Larry Keefauver provided tremendous insight and assistance in the editing of this book. Ana and I are thankful to him and his wonderful wife, Judi, for their friendship and example. Dave Hail added valuable counsel throughout the project. I am deeply thankful for the wise counsel and friendship of him and his wife, Janie.

Sarah Wolf invested countless hours and massive amounts of self-less energy into this book. It is a much better manuscript because of her diligence and spiritually sensitive insights. Vanessa Coenraad "midwifed" this book through its birth, pushing where we needed pushing and praying where we needed prayer. Her contagious love for the Lord and loyal friendship is a treasured gift. Peter Ecenroad did a fantastic job on the graphics and cover design. Peter is truly a "son of David" who is serving the purpose of God in this generation. To all the others who prayed, read the manuscript, offered comments and criticisms, and gave encouragement, thank you! May the Lord be pleased to use this book as an acceptable sacrifice for His Kingdom's sake.

Robert Stearns
New York City
Erev Yom Kippur, 5764
October 5, 2003

FOREWORD

As one who has known Robert Stearns as his Pastor, and as one who has helped to father him in the faith, it is my honor to now express my confidence in his leadership, anointing and personal integrity. Our relationship over the past fifteen years has given me a close, personal perspective as I have observed the expanding leadership he has leant to the Body of Christ.

Keepers of the Flame is a book that I believe is a "prophetic picture" of the Church that God desires to build during these last days in the earth. It is a book that makes demands on the reader to take action, and make decisions. Although the book seems at first to be written to individual believers, it is, I believe, a call to every pastor and church leader to examine a new paradigm of God's Church.

Interestingly, Robert Stearns, who is one of the world's most dynamic worship leaders, does not write about how to do worship, or how to develop one's church into a worshipping body of believers. He does not mention methodology or liturgical expressions of worship. Rather, he speaks of how to develop a lifestyle of worship that is "acceptable to God."

I had the privilege of being raised as a child in an Assemblies of God church during the 1930's. During those days, my father managed the cafeterias in four of those early camp meetings every summer. In this atmosphere I had the opportunity to hear the teaching of the greatest Assemblies of God Bible teachers of that generation. I sat every day for dinner at the table with such Bible teachers as Allen Swift, Hattie Hammond and John Wright Folette. Contrary to many of the contemporary evangelical movements, they pictured a glorious end-time Church, which would experience the greatest revival in Church

history. I personally believe that my forefathers had a prophetic revelation of what God was about to do in their world.

The Church they pictured was a Church who would become a
mature body of believers, in contrast to the immaturity of the present Church. They further examined the Scriptures and discovered
that Christ would return for a Church without spot or wrinkle.
Thirdly, they talked about how this Church of revival would produce
a class of people who would manifest the true nature of the sons of
God. After fifty years of ministry since I heard these teachers, I have
observed a Church that was not mature, was not without spot or
wrinkle and surely was not a manifestation of the true sons of God
on the earth. My question is, if this great move of God is coming to
our earth, how will it happen?

Church leaders flock by the thousands to leadership and church
growth conferences where the hope to discover how to make their
church grow, flourish and become successful. We have developed
terms to describe the models of successful churches such as 'seeker
sensitive church,' 'renewal church,' 'apostolic church' or 'multi-cul-
tural church.' With the latest techniques, the use of power point,
videos and drama, we are presented with the methods and models of
tomorrow's Church.

But *Keepers of the Flame* warns us that when we pursue numbers
and personal success, we also present a Gospel that elevates the 'self
interests' in the very people we are attempting to reach. The author
states, "A consumer-based Christianity which believes that a nice,
self-fulfilled American life is what Jesus came to give, must be broken
through."

He then proceeds to present a Biblical paradigm for tomorrow's model of the Church; a model that could produce this end-time Church of maturity. It is a model that tears at the core of a leader's heart, as he examines the purposes of God for His church. The paradigm he presents is a Church who declares the rule and reign of Christ manifested on the earth through a mature group of believers who have learned not to just worship God in the corporate body, but who live a "lifestyle of worship."

The first concept the book presents as the author describes a body of believers who learn to live a "lifestyle of worship," is the process of building an altar. The contemporary altar is described as 'living stones,' or the building of covenant relationships between people. He speaks of the "relational interaction in the place worship."

I was personally moved to ask myself the question, "Have I built this kind of a relational altar in the church where I pastor, or have I succumbed to the traditional, corporate model of the Church?"

The second part of this book deals with "The Sacrifice." Here in this section we are challenged both individually and corporately to a Kingdom lifestyle of sacrifice and self-denial. No one can read this section of the book without hearing the convicting voice of God as we are challenged to bring our lives as a living sacrifice on the altar.

The final section of the book deals with "The Fire." I quote from Chapter 15: "There is nothing in Scripture that tells us that God is anything less than an aggressive invader who demands all or nothing, hot or cold. The confrontation of His flame presents a choice, 'Choose you this day, whom you will serve' (Joshua 24:15)."

I could not read this section of the book without feeling the passion that God has placed in my heart for His Presence and His Fire.

As a fellow "renewalist," I hear the passion of Robert Stearns as he sees the key to seeing massive change in the Church is taking off all controls and letting the Fire of the Spirit come to bring that change first to our lives, and then to the world around us.

In the pages of this challenging book, I have found, and I pray that leaders of the Church will find a model for their own lives, and the life of the church of tomorrow. Perhaps in this profound manuscript, Robert Stearns has discovered for all of us the bridge that we must cross to fulfill the mandate of Scripture to build a mature body of believers who will be truly a manifestation of Jesus Christ on the earth.

Pastor Tommy Reid
The Tabernacle
Buffalo, NY

AN ACCEPTABLE SACRIFICE

Is God hearing us?

I realize the question is a bit silly. Of course He is hearing us. He is God.

I don't mean, '*Can* God hear us?'—God is omniscient and knows our words before they are formed on our lips. I am not questioning God's willingness or ability to hear us. My question has more to do with the sound we're making than the One to whom we're making the sound.

Are we saying or doing anything to evoke a divine response?

Is our worship touching the One we're worshipping?

Are we praying prayers and living lives that *reach His heart* and *move His hand?*

ARE WE AS A PEOPLE —THE BODY OF CHRIST AS A WHOLE IN THIS GENERATION— SEEKING GOD BUT NOT REALLY FINDING HIM?

Are there qualifications for God to respond?

Are we as a people—the Body of Christ as a whole in this generation—seeking God but not really finding Him? Is our intercession connecting with the God of the universe or merely broadcasting religious words into an empty void of our own imaginations and dreams?

I know *He* is present . . . *but are we?*

We have been consistently taught of the benevolence and nearness of God. We have been repeatedly been made aware of His lovingkindness and readiness to forgive, pardon, heal and help.

You may have sung the familiar song, "We Bring the Sacrifice of Praise." If you were raised in Christian settings similar to my upbringing, then you have sung this song hundreds, if not thousands of times. It is a wonderful song that encourages us to come before the Lord with joy and thanksgiving.

But as I read the Scripture, I have been impacted by the numerous times that God admonishes us not just to bring a sacrifice, but to bring **an acceptable sacrifice**.

Are we? Are we bringing an acceptable sacrifice to the Lord in this generation?

Instead of bringing whatever we feel like bringing to the Lord, whenever and however we choose, what if there were principles and guidelines set in place that caused our intercession to be more than just words?

In fact, there are many instances in Scripture in which qualifications are given in order for God to respond; principles and guidelines specify the ways in which God desires to be worshipped. But all too often, what God calls acceptable worship, we deem too demanding, too offensive, too undignified and even too impious to tolerate with our rational sensibilities.

Is the sacrifice of praise and worship, prayer and offerings we're bringing to the Lord really acceptable to God, or simply pleasing and comfortable for us?

I ask this because I am confused. I am very confused about something that seems out of order—something that seems not to make sense.

God has said that if we would call, He would answer. And everywhere, all around the world, there is a tremendous call going up to the Lord. Prayer meetings are happening like never before. Houses of Prayer are springing up in cities across the world. Contemporary worship has become mainstream in most Christian circles. Worship conferences, rallies, prayer gatherings, spiritual mapping, spiritual warfare conferences and reconciliation journeys multiply exponentially around us.

Nonetheless, what these have produced is not a great outpouring from Heaven, but rather an ever-increasing hunger for more of the same. Why? *In the midst of all of this wonderful activity, what is the condition of the people of God?*

George Barna has made some interesting observations regarding the current state of the Church and our ability to really connect with God through acceptable sacrifice:

Barna notes these paradoxes:

- Less than 10% of church members give a tithe (10% of their income).
- A large majority of Christians contend that there is no absolute, moral truth.
- More than half of those attending church on any given weekend do not trust Christ for their eternal salvation.
- Seven out of ten Christians (70%) say they have never experienced God's presence at a church service.

The comfort of our buildings and material possessions have misled us into believing we're further down the road in changing our world for Christ than we really are.

Why is this? Why do we hear every day about another "church split," another moral failure, another divorce, another pastor leaving the ministry or another Christian brother or sister falling into sin? Why, behind the scenes of the successful American Church, does it seem that we are poor, naked and very, very sick?

WHY, BEHIND THE SCENES OF THE SUCCESSFUL AMERICAN CHURCH, DOES IT SEEM THAT WE ARE POOR, NAKED AND VERY, VERY SICK?

I do not pretend to have all the answers. This book does not offer all the answers. But what I am hoping to do is ask some penetrating questions, which will move us off the merry-go-round of fruitless religious activity and point us in the direction of biblical discipleship. In other words, it's time to return to doing the *main thing*—**worshipping Jesus**. Any other lukewarm substitute, God spits out of His mouth.

Let us discover that:

- An acceptable sacrifice to God does exist and we can offer it.
- Prayer can and will be answered by the God who changes us and history.
- Worship will usher in God's presence in such a way that what the early Church experienced of God we will experience— in greater measure!

If you desire to become who God created you to be by living a life of acceptable worship, join me on this journey. Become a *keeper of the flame* and burn with the Presence of the Living God.

I walked with the rest of the tourists into the huge, cavernous building, our footsteps and muted voices echoing off the enormous stone
walls, stone floor and impressive pillars. Light poured in through the
stained glass windows, warming the glow of the wooden pews. The
building looked very much like one of the impressive cathedrals of
Europe; except that this was Australia, and we weren't in a church. We
were in the Great Synagogue of Sydney, Australia.

As the guide began to share with our group the history of the
Jewish community in Australia, my eyes were drawn to a light, shining in a lamp, hanging in the very center of the altar area. I had seen
these before in Synagogues in Israel, and thought it interesting that I
would see one here also, in a place so far away from Israel, both geo-
graphically and culturally.

During the question and answer time, I asked the guide about
the lamp.

"This is the *nair tamid*," he said. "This is the everlasting light that
you will find in every synagogue, hanging over the altar area. It is
wired directly into the electricity, so that the light never goes out. The
light represents the mandate that was given to our people through
Moses," he continued, "that the holy fire that has been entrusted to
the children of Israel must never go out. It represents the burnt offerings that used to be offered up at the Temple."

As the tour concluded and we meandered around the building,
getting a last look at things, I marveled at the *nair tamid*, and deeply
considered what it represented. What other people group or culture
has customs and traditions that they have kept for 5000 years? What
was it about this commissioning regarding the flame that so embed-

ded itself in the corporate Jewish consciousness that here, thousands of miles away and thousands of years later, this Jewish community—and indeed, all Jewish communities in the world—still endeavor to honor the mandate they received?

And finally, what was the relationship between the enduring tenacity of the Jewish community, which has survived against all odds for thousands of years; and the flame of the knowledge of God, which has remained burning for thousands of years, and until the time of Paul, was kept by their community alone?

Time and time again in biblical history, the Jewish people (and thus the knowledge of the One True God, the God of Abraham, Isaac, and Jacob) could have vanished from the earth. Whether it was the exile into Babylon, or the crisis during the time of Queen Esther, there were countless opportunities for the Jewish people to give up, to assimilate, to stop clinging to their faith and the culture which flows from that faith. Yet, a remnant of the Jewish people never gave up, even at unbelievable personal cost, many times at the cost of their lives.

Jewish mothers lit Sabbath candles in their homes on Erev Shabbat, to welcome the Sabbath, even if it meant danger to their families. They kept the flame alive. And, so, the flame has kept them alive. No other culture can trace its history and testimony for so many millennia in the earth. No other people group has been so small, faced so much hatred, and yet has not only survived, but has prospered in every land, in every generation. From Israel to Australia and back to Israel again, they traveled, and the flame came with them.

They have kept the flame, and so the flame has kept them. It has *preserved* them as a people and *defined* them as a culture.

Back to Basics

As I considered these things, I wondered what this meant for us, the "wild olive branch" who have been grafted into the covenants of God with Abraham. What was, and is, God's intent for His people in the earth? Since we as the Church are now, by faith, a part of God's people (Gal. 3:7), we need to ask ourselves what our primary calling is. Still today, God is looking for His people to be a "light to the nations."

Are we shining? Are we carrying that Light? Are we tending the Flame?

This book examines the call on the people of God to be, primarily and fundamentally, *a covenant community of worshippers*—to be a people in covenant with God and with one another—with our priority being to live individual and corporate lifestyles of worship and prayer. God is still looking for a "resting place". He still "inhabits the praises of His people." He is ever-longing for the knowledge

HE IS EVER-LONGING FOR THE KNOWLEDGE AND PRESENCE OF THE HOLY TO INVADE THE EARTHLY AND MUNDANE, AS THOSE WHO ARE CALLED BY HIS NAME CRY OUT TO HIM NIGHT AND DAY.

and presence of the Holy to invade the earthly and mundane, as those who are called by His name cry out to Him night and day. He is looking for a "royal priesthood" who will offer up acceptable sacrifices that capture His attention and move Him to action.

We, as believers in the God of Abraham, Isaac and Jacob, through Jesus, have been grafted into this calling to be *keepers of the flame*. We must receive this mandate as our own. And we must examine afresh in this generation how well we are tending that which has been entrusted to us. We must *refocus* our attention, *remember* our priority and *recapture* our purpose. We must pay for our beliefs with our lifestyle; a lifestyle that reflects a divine priority. We must receive that priority so strongly and so thoroughly that it burns its way into our collective consciousness so that, like the Jewish people, wherever we go and whatever we do, our prime directive is clear.

We must be *keepers of the flame*.

THE CALL

As a prisoner for the Lord, then,
I urge you to live a life worthy of the calling
you have received.

EPHESIANS 4:1

CHAPTER 1

A KINGDOM OF WORSHIPPERS

Before we are called to anything—before we are called to preach, pro-phesy, raise the dead or win the lost, we are called to be worshippers.

The first question posed in the Westminster Catechism is, "What is the chief end of man?" The answer given is simply this:

**Man's chief end is to glorify God,
and to enjoy Him forever.**

But why are we to worship? Is it simply to make us feel good or to make God feel good?

NO! When we worship God ACCEPTABLY, things happen!

When people worshipped in Scripture, God responded. As Israel worshipped at the base of Mt. Sinai, God showed up in power and grace. As Joshua and the people of God marched around Jericho in worship and praise, the enemy's walls came tumbling down.

As Solomon with the whole nation worshipped in dedicating the

Temple, God's glory came with such power that no one could stand. A solitary prophet named Elijah cried out to God in prayerful wor-

TIME AFTER TIME, WE SEE THAT THE RIGHT CONDITION OF ONE'S HEART, EVIDENCED BY ONE'S ACTIONS AND LIFESTYLE, MOVES THE HAND OF GOD.

ship and fire fell from heaven.

As the disciples and followers of Jesus gathered to pray and worship after Jesus' ascension, the Holy Spirit poured out from heaven at Pentecost. As the Church prayed and worshipped, God sent an angel to set Peter free from prison.

God responds to acceptable worship. Acceptable worship results in divine, supernatural response.

Scripture records the faithfulness of God. When we consider the mighty acts of God, His miracles and judgments, we see an undeniable connection between His deeds and our deeds; a connection between our *actions* and His *response*. The Living God desires relationship with us and always seeks to share His heart with those willing to listen. Time after time, we see that the right condition of one's heart, evidenced by one's actions and lifestyle, moves the hand of God. When we deliberately choose to give our lives to praise, obedience, sacrifice and devotion; the Kingdom of God draws near.

Scriptural Precedents

The children of Israel experienced this truth in a powerful way as they engaged in their battle for the Promised Land. By focusing on bringing honor to God and ignoring how ridiculous their antics must have seemed to their enemies, they defeated their foe and received the promise.

Then the LORD said to Joshua, "See, I have delivered Jericho into your hands, along with its king and its fighting men. March *around the city once with all the armed men. Do this for six days. Have seven priests carry trumpets of rams' horns in front of the ark. On the seventh day, march around the city seven times, with the priests blowing the trumpets. When you hear them sound a long blast on the trumpets, have all the people give a loud shout; then the wall of the city will collapse and the people will go up, every man straight in." On the seventh day, they got up at daybreak and marched around the city seven times in the same manner, except that on that day they circled the city seven times. The seventh time around, when the priests sounded the trumpet blast, Joshua commanded the people, "Shout! For the LORD has given you the city! When the trumpets sounded, the people shouted, and at the sound of the trumpet, when the people gave a loud shout, the wall collapsed; so every man charged straight in, and they took the•ity* (Joshua 6:2-5, 15-16, 20).*

In seeking to please God by doing *exactly* what was required of them, Joshua and his army accomplished the impossible. *They based their actions on what God wanted, and not on what the situation seemed to dictate.* This serves as an irrevocable precedent linking praise to warfare, and obedience to response.

God brings the victory not when we strive, but when we praise. Acceptable praise and worship triumph over any hindering circumstances or situations.

Worship is a Choice

All worship begins with a choice. In every situation, we are given the choice of how to respond to the circumstances we face. We can act out of our natural feelings or we can choose to deny our flesh and our natural understanding, and worship God.

Consider the choices of the early Church:

After they had been severely flogged, they were thrown into prison, and the jailer was commanded to guard them carefully. About midnight Paul and Silas were praying and singing hymns to God, and the other prisoners were listening to them. Suddenly there was such a violent earthquake that the foundations of the prison were shaken. At once all the prison doors flew open, and everybody's chains came loose (Acts 16:23-26).

IN OUR DAY, WORSHIP IS ALL TOO OFTEN THOUGHT OF AS A SONG SERVICE OF TWENTY TO THIRTY MINUTES ON SUNDAY MORNING. WE EVEN RATE WORSHIP!

Though Paul and Silas had reason enough to resent the circumstances they were in; they nonetheless chose to praise the Lord instead of becoming bitter. They could have cried out to God in any number of ways—anger, despair or defiance. Yet, they were so in love with His Presence that they found it within themselves to obey His command to give thanks in all things.

Their obedience resulted in their deliverance. Out of their worship and praise, God moved and victory resulted. *Keepers of the flame* are willing to praise God and fully abandon themselves in worship no matter what prison of circumstances they find themselves in.

Fully-Abandoned Worship

So much of the time, there is a temptation to rationalize our offerings and our worship. We are tempted to give what will appear acceptable in the eyes of others, rather than what will truly please God. We can be more motivated by fear of man than by a desire to please our Lord.

When we come to the Lord in sincerity and humility, giving not what we think we can afford, *but giving what we know we cannot afford to withhold,* we touch our Father's heart. An event near the end of Jesus' life reveals the value He places on *fully-abandoned worship.*

> *While he was in Bethany, reclining at the table in the home of a man known as Simon the Leper, a woman came with an alabaster jar of very expensive perfume, made of pure nard. She broke the jar and poured the perfume on his head. Some of those present were saying indignantly to one another, "Why this waste of perfume? It could have been sold for more than a year's wages and the money given to the poor." And they rebuked her harshly. "Leave her alone," said Jesus. "Why are you bothering her? She has done a beautiful thing to me. I tell you the truth, wherever the gospel is preached throughout the world, what she has done will also be told, in memory of her"* (Mark 14:3-6,9).

Expecting nothing in return, and ignoring the scorn of the crowd, this woman poured her most valuable possession on the body of Jesus. She received the honor of having her deed recorded in Scripture. What a blessing she would have missed had she listened to the voices in the background, and not given her all in worship!

What this woman did went against all decorum and common sense. And Jesus loved her act of fully-abandoned worship. Those around her (and us) may be intent on performing empty, religious activity based on human reason, and will therefore always scorn true acts of devotion. But Jesus sees completely through selfish and self-centered ritual posing as worship. He says, *"Yet a time is coming and has now come when the true worshippers will worship the Father in spirit and truth, for they are the kind of worshippers the Father seeks. God is spirit, and his worshippers must worship in spirit and in truth"* (John 4:23-24).

Jesus is always touched by acts of true worship in which a person, like the woman who anointed Jesus with costly perfume, commits himself or herself to fully-abandoned worship. The Lord is touched by extravagant offerings, and will bless us beyond our ability to bless Him.

Whole-Hearted Worship

Jesus reminds us of our priority by reiterating the greatest commandment: "*Love the Lord your God with **all your heart** and with all your soul and with all your mind*" (Matt. 22:37, emphasis added).

Living before God requires much more than attending a service for an hour or two every week. We must show our love for the Lord by giving Him everything; by giving Him the very lifestyle we live. We see, for example, through the life of Anna, that a sacrifice which is costly to the bearer is a sacrifice that God accepts.

> *On the eighth day, when it was time to circumcise him, he was named Jesus, the name the angel had given him before he had been conceived. When the time of their purification according to the Law of Moses had been completed, Joseph and Mary took him to Jerusalem to present him to the Lord (as it is written in the Law of the Lord, "Every firstborn male is to be consecrated to the Lord"), and to offer a sacrifice in keeping with what is said in the Law of the Lord: "a pair of doves or two young pigeons."*
>
> *There was also a prophetess, Anna, the daughter of Phanuel, of the tribe of Asher. She was very old; she had lived with her husband seven years after her marriage, and then was a widow until she was eighty-four. She never left the temple but worshiped night and day, fasting and praying. Coming up to them at that very moment, she gave thanks to God and spoke about the child to all who were looking forward to the redemption of Jerusalem* (Luke 2:21-24, 36-38).

Instead of pursuing her right to a comfortable life by re-marrying someone who would provide for her needs, Anna chose a lifestyle of disciplined temple worship. Her faith-filled choices and her constant, selfless giving pleased God. The Lord rewarded Anna's lifetime of devotion by allowing her to see with her own eyes the One who would redeem Israel.

So often, we cry out in worship to "see God." Only the pure in heart see God. That purity of heart arises out of a passionate love for Him. That's loving God wholeheartedly.

Fully-abandoned, whole-hearted worship involves more than a weekly commitment to attending a worship service. In our day, worship is all too often thought of as a song service of twenty to thirty minutes on Sunday morning. We even rate worship! "He's a great worship leader!" "That fellowship has a wonderful worship team!"

My friend, can worship be separated from our lifestyle?

If worship is our sacrifice, isn't it possible that it is deemed *acceptable* or *unacceptable* by the quality of our lifestyle, as opposed to the quality of our musicianship?

Corporately, is it possible that much of the Body of Christ is engaged in an abundance of religious activity, but very little *acceptable worship* is being offered? I suggest that this is one of the reasons why we are seeing little if any results of biblical proportion taking place in the Western Church today.

Is it possible that we are largely involved in "doing church" instead of living Christian discipleship?

You might say "Robert, our church is doing great! We have just completed a huge building program and we are packed on Sunday mornings!"

So?

Beloved, we cannot measure success in God's Kingdom by the standards of Babylon. Since when are numbers a standard of biblical,

Kingdom success? Large crowds must never become our primary indicator of achievement in our work for the Lord.

Keepers of the Flame Don't Measure Success in Numbers

From cover to cover, the Bible is the story of God's interaction with a *remnant*. Over and over again we see that the *keepers of the flame* were not in the majority. Instead, God had to find a remnant in the midst of the community who were willing to live lifestyles of extravagant worship and obedience, no matter what.

Consider Gideon. 32,000 people showed up to fight for the Lord with Gideon. But God said, "*The people who are with you are too many* . . . " (Judges 7:2a NKJV, emphasis added). So God tested the people and showed Gideon that he must send 22,000 people away, leaving only 10,000.

Imagine a popular, high-profile leader today having over thirty thousand people show up, and that leader sends two-thirds of them away before even beginning the service! That leader would be considered crazy. But that's what God told Gideon to do . . . and even more! God put the people through another test and only 300 remained to fight the battle. Less than one percent of the original number was found acceptable!

Gideon may have felt secure and safe in his own strength with a great crowd to serve God. But God was looking for a few, committed servants who would fight, persevere and trust Him for the battle's victory. Such thinking really goes against our conventional wisdom, but it was right on in God's sight.

Here we see that God so values Gideon's sole dependence on Him, that He goes out of His way to prove that battles are won by God, not by man. God's instructions to Gideon (which were totally irrational and contradictory to good military tactics), clearly lay out God's value system. The Creator of the universe does not need anything we can give Him. But He loves when we give Him our very selves by laying our reputation on the line and taking a leap of faith.

Like Gideon, when our hearts trust in God instead of in our own ability to succeed, we are then ready to receive from the Lord. God delights in defying human logic and strength by causing victory to break forth in the most unlikely of circumstances.

Consider Jesus. A huge crowd showed up to worship and praise God as Jesus entered Jerusalem on a donkey. The large crowd cried out:

> *"Hosanna to the Son of David!"*
> *"Blessed is he who comes in the name of the Lord!"*
> *"Hosanna in the highest!"* (Matthew 21:9).

What awesome praise! What an exciting start to worship! Jesus' disciples must have felt a huge, emotional rush by such a large, enthusiastic crowd. It seemed like an impressive launch for a successful, triumphal ministry for Jesus.

Today, such a start to a big meeting or worship event would thrill the numbers-oriented leader. Having a huge crowd shouting to the Lord always produces great religious energy, but it's no guarantee of fully-abandoned, wholehearted worship.

Remember that by the end of the week, that same crowd and the disciples had all abandoned worship and turned

HAVING A HUGE CROWD SHOUTING TO THE LORD ALWAYS PRODUCES GREAT RELIGIOUS ENERGY, BUT IT'S NO GUARANTEE OF FULLY-ABANDONED, WHOLEHEARTED WORSHIP.

against the Son of God. Instead of shouts of praise, their shouts had become, *"Crucify him!"* (John 19:15a).

Consider Paul. This man murdered Christians. When he finally repented and turned to Christ, he alienated some of the core leadership of the early Church. He found powerful groups of believers opposing his mission to the Gentiles. And the religious Jewish leaders of the day (of which he was one) persecuted, mocked, beat, imprisoned and sought to kill him.

Where did his fully-abandoned life to Christ take him? Just read a brief description of what his life following Jesus was like:

> *Five times I received from the Jews the forty lashes minus one. Three times I was beaten with rods, once I was stoned, three times I was shipwrecked, I spent a night and a day in the open sea, I have been constantly on the move. I have been in danger from rivers, in danger from bandits, in danger from my own countrymen, in danger from Gentiles; in danger in the city, in danger in the country, in danger at sea; and in danger from false brothers. I have labored and toiled and have often gone without sleep; I have known hunger and thirst and have often gone without food; I have been cold and naked* (2 Cor. 11:24-27).

If one were to measure Kingdom success by worldly standards, the life of the Apostle Paul might present some difficulty. Not only did Paul lack worldly esteem and recognition; at times, he didn't even have a core of believers to stand with him. How would Paul be received in the Church today?

No doubt, Paul would be dismissed by many who insist on judging the spiritual by the natural. Yet from this one man, who would seem so easy to dismiss, we have many New Testament epistles, as well as having a firm foundation of the early Church. Listen to Paul's words to Timothy.

> *Do your best to come to me quickly, for Demas, because he loved this world, has deserted me and has gone to Thessalonica. Crescens has gone to Galatia, and Titus to Dalmatia. Only Luke is with*

me. Get Mark and bring him with you, because he is helpful to me in my ministry. Alexander the metalworker did me a great deal of harm. The Lord will repay him for what he has done. At my first defense, no one came to my support, but everyone deserted me. May it not be held against them (2 Tim. 4:9-11,14,16).

As Paul implored Timothy to join him, we see that he was not concerned with the *number of men* he had, but with having the *one man* who was right for the job. In no way does Paul care about recovering those who have deserted him. Even though Paul obviously feels the loss of those who chose to leave, his words indicate that the others' decisions are the Lord's responsibility. He is not worried about how things look, but instead is concerned with God's will being fulfilled. Paul must have understood the principle of godly remnant: ***to accomplish the Lord's work, you need only what the Lord gives you.***

THE CHURCH IS A LIVING COMMUNITY OF COVENANTAL RELATIONSHIPS CENTERED AROUND PRAYER AND WORSHIP, OUT OF WHICH ANOINTED SERVICE FLOWS.

Quality not Quantity in Worship

Throughout His Word, God makes it clear that He values quality over quantity. Do you recall a place in Scripture where God was impressed by man's resources? Was God ever compelled to act because people looked like they had it all together?

On the contrary, the Lord even goes so far as to deliberately destroy the appearance of fleshly strength, *"For the foolishness of God is wiser than man's wisdom, and the weakness of God is stronger than man's strength"* (1 Cor. 1:25).

Gideon's first army of 30,000 must have been an awesome sight. The Passover crowd praising Jesus must have thrilled His followers.

The impressive ministry of Paul, which fueled the growth of the burgeoning Church, must have seemed extremely exciting to those who experienced its momentum.

The life of Jesus is the ultimate example of achieving Kingdom success using only the power of God. By seeking no affirmation from the world, and utilizing no strength of His own, Jesus was exalted above all the earth and overcame death for all time. The One to whom all authority is given in heaven and on earth and under the earth did not desire it from these places. Rather, by enduring complete rejection and abandonment, even by His Heavenly Father as He bore our sins on the cross, Jesus secured our eternal redemption. Because of this, we too can base our identity not on the world's systems of success, but on God's Kingdom values.

We cannot measure success by how many people come to our Easter cantatas or fill our buildings on Sunday because of our fantastic children's programs. This is not Christianity. This is consumerism.

The Church is not a building where people attend a meeting. The Church is a living community of covenantal relationships centered around prayer and worship, out of which anointed service flows.

Every one of us has known of mega churches and large ministries that collapse in a day because there is no structural integrity to them. They seem strong and secure, but they are built on the strength of man rather than the strength of God; and when the winds blow, they are revealed for the hollow shell that they are.

We must base our success on how much biblical discipleship is happening in our midst; not how many people are attracted to us, how much money flows into the ministry or how many buildings we can build. Instead, we must begin in a life of fully-abandoned worship to live out Kingdom values in Kingdom reality. We must become a kingdom of worshippers: *"You will be for me a kingdom of priests and a holy nation"* (Exod. 19:6a).

How does that happen? We can now look at the pattern of worship as seen in the Old Testament. Discover with me essential principles that I believe can help serve as guidelines for us today in our search for authentic worship that is acceptable to God because it flows out of a wholehearted, abandoned lifestyle, pleasing to Him.

Keys for Keepers of the Flame

- Focus on authentic heart issues in worship.
- Decide to abandon yourself fully and wholeheartedly in loving worship of Jesus.
- Make fully-abandoned worship a lifestyle, not a once-a-week experience.
- Decide that true worship is worth whatever sacrifice and cost you must offer to God.
- Give up the ritual of just attending religious meetings and begin a lifestyle of daily meeting with God.

THE BURNT OFFERING

*The L*ORD *said to Moses: "Give Aaron and his sons this command: 'These are the regulations for the burnt offering: The burnt offering is to remain on the altar hearth throughout the night, till morning, and **the fire must be kept burning on the altar**. The priest shall then put on his linen clothes, with linen undergarments next to his body, and shall remove the ashes of the burnt offering that the fire has consumed on the altar and place them beside the altar. Then he is to take off these clothes and put on others, and carry the ashes outside the camp to a place that is ceremonially clean. **The fire on the altar must be kept burning**; it must not go out. Every morning the priest is to add firewood and arrange the burnt offering on the fire and burn the fat of the fellowship offerings on it. **The fire must be kept burning on the altar continuously**; it must not go out.*

LEVITICUS 6:8-13, EMPHASIS ADDED

CHAPTER 2

ANCIENT FIRE, ENDURING FLAME

The call on Israel to keep the flame day and night was a national call. It came to the whole nation, and determined their national priority. In walking out that mandate, some of the functional responsibilities fell to the tribe of Levi.

The members of the tribe of Levi were called to be priests of the children of Israel. But it is essential for us as worshippers to understand that it's not enough to have the office, or position, of priest. Occupying the office of priest requires a particular priority, an essential demand, and an ongoing mandate.

Let's examine this thought for a moment. An office may exist in theory, but in reality an office never exists without function. The office of President exists in the Constitution of the United States. But until someone occupies that office and acts with executive authority, there is no functioning executive head of government.

A car has been manufactured to move down the highway. Everything can be present—motor, gasoline, keys and every mechanical system ready to go. The engine can even be running. But without a driver the car goes nowhere.

A worship service may be planned, rehearsed and even started. People may even be assembled or gathered in a room called a sanc-

TO TRULY BE
A PRIEST OF THE
MOST HIGH GOD,
WE MUST
RENDER WORSHIP
UNTO HIM.

tuary. But worship never happens without true worshippers. Without those who have kept the flame . . . the passion . . . the fire of their hearts ablaze with the purpose of glorifying God—no worship occurs.

All the offices of the Church may be present—apostle, pastor, evangelist, prophet and teacher. But without worship, the offices are empty and their purposes unful-filled. What comes first? Apostle then prophet? How would the people even be there without the evangelist? Would they ever gather without the pastor? Could they ever know what to do without the teacher? Each office is important but not primary; essential, while not taking precedence over the others. Before the *office* necessarily comes the *function*—that which every office must be and do in order to be authentic.

What is the function of the office of priest? To truly be a priest of the Most High God, we must render *worship* unto Him. And all of us, together, are called to be a kingdom of priests.

We have already learned that worship is the very essence of our being, and is that which we were created to do. We know *what* worship is. Throughout the remainder of our time together, we will be examining *how* to worship God.

The premise of this book rests on God's instruction to ancient Israel on how to worship. Only by examining this timeless mandate can we, as those who believe in the God of Israel today, offer worship that is pleasing to Him.

The Ancient Fire

The LORD said to Moses: "Give Aaron and his sons this command: 'These are the regulations for the burnt offering: The burnt offering is to remain on the altar hearth throughout the night, till morning, and the fire must be kept burning on the altar'" (Lev. 6:8-9).

God's mandate for his people was that they become a nation of priests to continually honor and worship Him by offering up a burnt offering.

The Lord clearly dictates to Moses that this is not a one day a week experience. Nor is it something that can be done casually whenever the people feel like it. It is not a sacrifice that can be brought at any time. Rather, this sacrifice must be brought at *all times.*

"The Fire must be kept burning on the altar."

Three times God repeats this in this passage (Leviticus 6:9-13), making it abundantly clear to His people what His priority is for them: *keep the flame burning!*

They must tend the flame.

It cannot go out.

Day and night, they must be *keepers of the flame.*

Then and Now

When we study Scripture, we understand the "Law of First Mention." This Law of hermeneutics, or scriptural interpretation, tells us that the first time something is mentioned in Scripture lays the foundational understanding for that concept throughout all of Scripture. So, if we want to understand marriage, we look at the first mention of marriage. If we are to understand tithing, we look at the first mention of tithing.

Here, we are looking at worship. We are looking at the first times God calls for worship and sacrifice from His people.

I want you to think about your concept of worship. You probably think of your Sunday morning service. Worship is most likely tied in your mind with pictures of musical instruments, choruses and hymns and a worship leader.

THE "CHIEF END OF MAN" IS FOUND HERE AS THESE DESERT NOMADS LIGHT THEIR FIRES AND RECEIVE FROM THE HOLY ONE, BLESSED BE HIS NAME.

But can you see and understand as you read this passage that there is a *direct historic and spiritual link* between what we see here in Leviticus and what we do on Sunday mornings? In other words, there is a timeline stretching throughout five or six thousand years in which the ultimate ancestor of your "worship service" is the scene described in Leviticus six.

Aaron and his sons, the words of Moses, the altar, the sacrifice and the fire—all of these expressions have changed. They have morphed and transitioned into the various forms we associate with worship today. But the original desire and plan of God is right there: *the altar, the wood, the fire, the sacrifice, the priest and the sweet aroma to the Lord.*

The root system of worship of the true and living God, the "chief end of man," is found here as these desert nomads light their fires and receive from the Holy One, Blessed Be His Name. They have been given their corporate mandate as a nation: *to keep the fire of God burning,* and so have we.

A Flame that Endures

Since we too are called to truly worship the God of Abraham, Isaac and Jacob in everything we do, we must have a proper understanding of the elements of worship that God set forth in Leviticus. Again, let's look at our Scriptural injunction:

> *The LORD said to Moses "Give Aaron and his sons this command: 'These are the regulations for the burnt offering: The burnt offering is to remain on the altar hearth throughout the night, till morning, and the fire must be kept burning on the altar'"* (Lev. 6:8-9).

I want us to see three aspects that are present at this burnt offering. By examining these three things, which are essential for worship, we can find clues that will allow us to *unlock the ancient secret of an acceptable sacrifice.* In the coming pages, our aim will be to discover principles that can be applied to our own lives, both individually and corporately, which will enable us to offer a sacrifice that pleases God.

That acceptable sacrifice, which brought the children of Israel extraordinary favor and miraculous provision, will bring us the same, for we too worship the same God. He is willing and wanting again to raise up a people in the earth who are blessed and walking in the power of His favor.

And, I believe there is a quality of life available to the community of the redeemed that far exceeds the norm that we have experienced in the contemporary Church.

Furthermore, I believe that if we will begin to again lift up an acceptable sacrifice, we will once more see God respond to us today as He did in days of old.

We are created to worship. Essential to worship is this: *keep the flame burning!*

1. We will examine the **altars** of our lives—our hearts, our families, our congregations, as well as our cities and regions.
2. We will look deeply at the condition of the **sacrifices** we

have been offering the Lord, both individually and corporately.

3. And we will talk about the burning **flame** of God—with all of its warmth, healing, power and mystery.

As we examine these three aspects of the burnt offering, we will discover in the end the one God is most interested in.

Our goals in all of this are . . .

That the Lord would realign us with Himself

That we would rouse ourselves
from the slumber of spectator Christianity,
which is no Christianity at all

That we would consecrate ourselves—
individually, by families, and by congregations and cities—
for the purposes of God to be brought forth
in both this and coming generations

Our cry is that the Lord would raise up a generation of priestly intercessors who will stand with the High Priest, Christ Jesus, who is at this moment leading the great Last Days' Prayer Meeting before the throne of God.

Our prayer is that an acceptable sacrifice would again be lifted up that would move the heart and hand of God; that we would see God arise in our day and in our time!

THE ALTAR

You also, like living stones,
are being built into a spiritual house
to be a holy priesthood,
offering spiritual sacrifices acceptable to God
through Jesus Christ.

I PETER 2:5

From the time that Abram built an altar and called on the name of the Lord, to Jesus' offering of Himself on the altar of the cross, Scripture is the story of man's meeting with God at the place of the altar. The altar was never just about the physical place of the sacrifice, but about the full story surrounding what was taking place as man called upon Heaven for the intervention of God.

The Altar *Then*

As the place of worship, the altar provided the foundation on which the sacrifice was made. This structure created the context in which the sacrifice took place. The sacrifice did not take place just anywhere. An altar had to be prepared carefully, and in the location and manner decided by God.

> *"Thou shalt build the altar of Jehovah thy God of unhewn stones;
> and thou shalt offer burnt offerings thereon unto Jehovah thy
> God"* (Deut. 27:6 ASV).

In many places throughout the Old Testament, our attention is called
to the importance of strong altars, as here with the example of King
Manasseh.

> *Afterward he rebuilt the outer wall of the City of David, west of the
> Gihon spring in the valley, as far as the entrance of the Fish Gate
> and encircling the hill of Ophel; he also made it much higher. He
> stationed military commanders in all the fortified cities in Judah.*
>
> *He got rid of the foreign gods and removed the image from
> the temple of the LORD, as well as all the altars he had built on
> the temple hill and in Jerusalem; and he threw them out of the
> city.* **Then he restored the altar of the LORD and sacrificed
> fellowship offerings and thank offerings on it, and told
> Judah to serve the LORD, the God of Israel.** *The people, how-
> ever, continued to sacrifice at the high places, but only to the
> LORD their God* (2 Chron. 33:14-17, emphasis added).

Notice both the *vertical* and *horizontal* relationships involved. The
restoring of the altar included getting the whole of a nation involved.
God demanded both holiness and justice, *intimacy with Him* and
right relationships with others.

The Altar *now: Thoughts for Today*

One thing that the altar can refer to today is the relationships in our
lives. We do not live our lives in a vacuum of abstractions. Our lives
take place in a structure, a context. The level of integrity we maintain
in our relationships is what will determine the validity of our message,

and ultimately the quality of our worship.

In evangelical Christianity, we have emphasized one's personal relationship with God through Jesus Christ. This is a glorious and foundational truth. But the reality is that from beginning to end, the Bible is a book not only about man's personal walk with God, but also a person's walk with his fellow man.

The Bible tells countless stories about the purposes of God being either brought forth or aborted through people . . . family and friends . . . interacting with one another.

Consider what comes to mind when you think about these relationships . . .

Abraham and Lot.

Moses, Aaron and Miriam.

Joseph and his brothers.

David and Jonathan and Saul.

Ruth and Naomi.

Samson and Delilah.

Eli, Hophni, Phineas and Samuel.

Mary and Joseph.

Jesus and his parents.

Jesus and his twelve disciples.

Jesus and His close friends, Mary, Martha and Lazarus.

Jesus and his cousin John.

Paul, Barnabas and John Mark.

All of Scripture lets us know that God's interaction with mankind does not take place in some super-spiritual, mystical world in which people are on a mountain alone with God. Though biblical heroes certainly have those mountain top experiences, the reality of those experiences is tested and proven in the context of the relationships they walk in.

In other words, the reality of the condition of the relational altar of your life is what proves or disproves your walk with God and whatever message or anointing you feel you have.

Scripture likens our covenant relationship with God to marriage, while it compares our relationships with one another to that of community or family. Scripture is about covenant.

And covenant—simply put—is the sacred condition by which we understand and relate to God, ourselves and each other.

FROM BEGINNING TO END, THE BIBLE IS A BOOK NOT ONLY ABOUT MAN'S PERSONAL WALK WITH GOD, BUT ALSO A PERSON'S WALK WITH HIS FELLOW MAN.

Certainly, all of our relationships will fall short of perfection and will experience strain and difficulty. Jesus Himself went through trying times with those whom he loved. He went through seasons in which His parents and brothers did not understand His message. He went through frustration with His close friends, Mary and Martha, over the death of Lazarus (John 11:32-34). He went through a time when his cousin, who had been the one to announce his public ministry, began to doubt Him (Luke 7:20).

What's necessary to keep the flame burning in our lives is not perfect relationships, but treasuring and maturing in our relationships in the ways God requires. God values loving, truthful, intimate relationships; so must we!

God Values Relationship

God esteems relationship so highly that *He Himself* is a community—Father, Son and Holy Spirit. His crowning act of creation was to create *community* in the garden. It's interesting to note that God didn't just create *relationship*, he created *community*. Two is a relationship—God and Adam. But God said it was not good for Adam to be alone, and so he created Eve, thus establishing community.

Can it be that in all of our preaching and teaching about a personal relationship with God, we have failed to realize that the Scripture clearly teaches that no relationship with God is possible without walking out that relationship with others?

> *"By this all men will know that you are my disciples, if you love one another"* (John 13:35).

> *"Religion that God our Father accepts as pure and faultless is this: to look after orphans and widows . . ."* (James 1:27a).

> *"Suppose a brother or sister is without clothes and daily food. If one of you says to him, 'Go, I wish you well; keep warm and well fed,' but does nothing about his physical needs, what good is it?"* (James 2:15-16).

> *"Beloved, if God so loved us, we also ought to love one another"* (1 John 4:11 NKJV).

> *"Therefore, if you are offering your gift at the altar and there remember that your brother has something against you, leave your gift there in front of the altar. First go and be reconciled to your brother; then come and offer your gift"* (Matthew 5:23-24).

Notice that! There it is again: that concept of an *acceptable offering!*

But you may say, "My offerings can never be perfect; that's why Jesus came in the New Testament. He is my sacrifice and my acceptable offering."

But beloved, the above words were spoken *by* Jesus in Matthew five! He is telling us that we cannot bring a "sacrifice of praise," we cannot come into God's presence, we cannot expect our worship to be in spirit and in truth, we cannot present an acceptable sacrifice if our relationships are filled with conflict.

What would happen to the spiritual climate over cities and congregations if we simply heeded these words of Jesus?

How many congregations across America have been birthed in

THE STONES OF OUR ALTARS ARE "LIVING STONES," THE RELATIONSHIPS WE HAVE WITH GOD AND WITH OTHERS.

division and strife or through splits from other congregations, in which there has been no forgiveness, no healing and no reconciliation?

Yet we continue on as though God is obligated to hear us and accept our offerings. However, He clearly states that if we are not demonstrating reconciliation one to another by maintaining acceptable *altars*, we cannot expect our *sacrifices* to be accepted either!

How Are the Altars of Your Relationships?

So, the relationships of our lives form the altar upon which the daily sacrifice is offered. The altar is not constructed of tithing, erecting buildings, developing programs and conducting events—as important as those things are. The stones of our altars are "living stones," the relationships we have with God and with others.

Think for a moment about your altars of relationship:

The marriage altar of husband and wife.

The parenting altar of parents and children.

The family altar of mothers, fathers, children, grandchildren, aunts, uncles, cousins, nephews, nieces, etc.

The kingdom altar of godly friendships.

The church altar of those members of a body gathering in a local fellowship

The corporate altar of those in the larger Body of Christ—
city, regional, national and global.

The citizens' altar comprised of those
with whom you relate in society—work, recreation, politics, etc.

I am certain that upon reflection we could add many other types
of altars to this list. What is the one common denominator?

Relationship.

The state of these relationships dramatically affects our relationship with God. The intensity and intimacy of love in those relationships significantly draws us in or distances us from God. John reminds us in his letter that we cannot say we love God while we are
hating others.

Are your altars in decay? Don't simply look at your church atten-
dance, the number of conferences you've flocked to or the multitude
of times you've prayed or read your Bible. Instead, examine your
relationships.

What is the condition of your altars?

Will they stand the stressful and difficult tests inherent in all relationships?

Are your altars made of hay, wood and stubble or of living stones
refined in the fires of blazing love, intense forgiveness and dedicated
servanthood?

What is God requiring of you right now in regard to some of the
altars in your life?

CHAPTER 3

THE FOUR COURTS
A Journey into Covenant Relationships

We have now gained the biblical understanding that relationships serve as the basis of God's Kingdom. In order for that concept to become a part of our paradigm, we need to grasp what the nature of relationship is, and the fact that all relationships are not meant to be the same.

By properly understanding the different levels of relationship, we'll be able to see what is required of us in these various aspects of our lives. As you discover how best to approach the relationships that have been entrusted to you, keep in mind that the chief reason God calls us to live in harmony with each other is so that we can live in union with Him.

Temple Worship

In the Old Testament Tabernacle and Temple, sacrifice and prayer were offered up in four different courts. Each court was progressively more selective and less inclusive in those who could be present. Passing through the courts was, in a sense, drawing closer to God. The nearer one came to the Holy of Holies, the nearer one was to God.

Ultimately, only the High Priest could enter the Holy of Holies, at only one time a year. During that day, Yom Kippur—the day of Atonement, he would intercede for the nation and offer sacrifice for their sin.

For the Jews, the Tabernacle and Temple had three courts—the outer court, the inner court and the Holy of Holies. In Herod's day, the outermost part of Herod's Temple had an additional area, the Court of the Gentiles. For our purposes, we will consider all four:

- The Court of the Gentiles
- The Outer Court
- The Inner Court, or Holy Place
- The Holy of Holies

These courts and the journey through them from the common-place to the Holy can be a picture guide for us as we look at the journey into covenant relationships, not only with God, but also with people.

As I have examined and studied these courts, I have discerned principles that can inform our worship as *keepers of the flame*. These principles can best be understood as levels, which correspond to each of these four areas of worship and relationship.

- **Connection**—the Court of the Gentiles
- **Cooperation**—The Outer Court
- **Commitment**—The Inner Court, or Holy Place
- **Covenant**—The Holy of Holies

Connection: The Court of the Gentiles

The Court of the Gentiles was a place reserved for those who were outside the Covenant of Israel. It was designated for Gentiles so that they would be provided a place for drawing near to God. These righteous Gentiles were called "God-fearers."

This area could represent the relationships in your life that are the least intimate, probably with unbelievers or believers with whom you have a casual relationship. However, just because these relationships are not *intimate* does not mean they are not *important*. Actually, in some ways they are *very* important. The Lord consistently spoke to the Israelites about how they treated the foreigner and stranger in their midst. The Torah in Leviticus 19 reads, *"The alien living with you must be treated as one of your native-born. Love him as yourself, for you were aliens in Egypt. I am the LORD your God"* (Lev. 19:34).

Connecting with Kindness and Caring

Jesus, through the parable of the Good Samaritan, emphasized the urgency of considering how we treat those who to us are not "in faith" or in covenant with the living God. This parable is so interesting when we remember that to the Jews, the Samaritans were second class citizens. They were the racially outcast people of the day.

But as Jesus tells this story to a Jewish audience, He doesn't make the wounded man a Samaritan and emphasize the goodness of the Jewish priest in helping him. Rather, he makes the Samaritan the hero of the story!

> *Jesus said: "A man was going down from Jerusalem to Jericho, when he fell into the hands of robbers. They stripped him of his clothes, beat him and went away, leaving him half dead. A priest happened to be going down the same road, and when he saw the man, he passed by on the other side. So too, a Levite, when he came to the place and saw him, passed by on the other side. But*

*a Samaritan, as he traveled, came where the man was; and when
he saw him, he took pity on him. He went to him and bandaged
his wounds, pouring on oil and wine. Then he put the man on
his own donkey, took him to an inn and took care of him. The
next day he took out two silver coins and gave them to the
innkeeper. 'Look after him,' he said, 'and when I return, I will
reimburse you for any extra expense you may have.' Which of
these three do you think was a neighbor to the man who fell into
the hands of robbers?"* (Luke 10:30-36).

How are we, those of us in covenant relationship with God, treating those who are outside of covenant? I am gravely concerned about
the impression the Church makes on the world. It seems that most
unbelievers consider the Church to be an irrelevant place full of con-
demnation and judgment.

How are you perceived by those with whom you have a casual
connection?

Are you actively cultivating open doors of communication with
them? Are you stretching beyond your comfort zone, like Jesus did
and forced others to do when he talked to women of ill repute at
wells, tax collectors at parties and sinners, wherever they were?

These "Outer Court" people were not religious in any way. Yet
they were comfortable around Jesus; even allowing Him access to their
hearts because Jesus was able to minister the love of God to them.

Connecting with Good News

The Outer Court is also the place of evangelism. It is the place where
we are involved in our communities, actively reaching beyond the
four walls of the church so we can be salt and light.

Remember that we, as children of light and *keepers of the flame,* are not bearers of a light that scorches and burns people with judgmental or condemning words and actions. On the contrary, by speaking the truth in love, we are to approach those in the Outer Court with the love of the Father who is ever seeking to save the lost.

We are not blind to or tolerant of sinful actions, but we are open to accepting and loving sinners who need to hear the good news of God's desire to enter into covenant relationship with them. They are invited to enter into His court and His presence. That invitation often comes from and through us. We are the gatekeepers who open the way for outsiders, those alien to God's ways, to experience God's love and grace through our relationships with them.

I BELIEVE THE CHURCH WOULD STAY MUCH SHARPER AND BE MUCH MORE RELEVANT IF WE DID NOT SEE PEOPLE AS "PROJECTS" TO "GET SAVED", BUT AS FRIENDS WITH WHOM WE CAN SHARE THE LIFE OF GOD IN A NATURAL WAY AS WE WALK OUT OUR DAYS TOGETHER.

Think about this. What unbeliever are you actively cultivating a relationship with? In what community activity are you involved that is putting you into regular, growing relationship with those you can share God with?

I believe the Church would stay much sharper and be much more relevant if we did not see people as "projects" to "get saved", but as friends with whom we can share the *life* of God in a natural way as we walk out our days together. I am thankful for evangelism programs and the success they *do* have, but lifestyle evangelism remains the *most effective* way for true conversions and meaningful discipleship to take place.

These relationships must begin in the place of the Court of the Gentiles. We must take the initiative and be intentional about seeking out such relationships.

Cooperation: The Outer Court

This level of interaction refers to people in your life with whom you have a casual, but ongoing connection. Those you might consider acquaintances, or with whom you would say you are friendly, but not necessarily friends.

These are other believers who have a personal relationship with Jesus Christ. However, while they are in the same family of God as you are, you simply do not know them well. You may sit next to them in a worship service and know their names. You may exchange polite greetings and superficial information with them, but how they live their lives outside your casual contact with them is not known to you.

We might even greet these persons that we see only intermittently with a, "Hi, friend." It is interesting that in American English, we so often use the word *friend* very flippantly and loosely. If we have met someone more than a few times, we are apt to call them our friend. This is not the case in other parts of the world.

In French, the word *acquaintance* is commonly used for people who are just that. If you were introducing two people, you might say, "John, meet Mary. She is an acquaintance of mine from school." The relationship is then defined as a casual relationship.

We cooperate with these fellow believers on certain projects and outreaches. We may work side by side at a church work day or picnic. We may go on a neighborhood prayer walk with them in the same team. But our cooperation is based on what we do together in a non-threatening, non-confrontational way. Outside of structured encounters like worship, a Sunday school class, a special church event or a planned activity, we never meet.

In the Outer Court, our relationship with Christ draws us into proximity with one another for the purpose of *doing* something together, corporately. But true knowledge of each other's values, hopes, dreams and aspirations is lacking. True intimacy that allows us to rejoice when they rejoice and hurt when they hurt doesn't yet exist.

This may become most evident when a time of worship invites those who are in deep need to stand or come forward for ministry or prayer. At that moment, the believer we have often spoken to or sat near in services, bursts into tears and rises for ministry. We are surprised. They have always seemed so "together" and so pleasant. Yet something within them was hidden from us because our relationship with them had been limited to *doing* something with them instead of *being* in a covenant relationship. Such a relationship requires more than cooperation; it requires commitment!

Commitment: The Inner Court

Now we have come to the place where we really are moving into relationships that are serious. These are significant relationships that have worth and meaning in your life.

To whom are you committed?

What relationships are you pouring time and energy into?

What value system frames and undergirds your understanding of relationships?

For whom would you lay down your life? Jesus indicates that true friends lay down their lives for one another. *"Greater love has no one than this, than to lay down one's life for his friends"* (John 15:13 NKJV). Such friendship means more than a willingness to physically die for a person. Each moment we live, we die to that moment. Time is a process of dying one second at a time. So when we spend our time with another person, we are, in a sense, dying for them. When we spend our time serving, honoring and even protecting the character of a friend against rumors or gossip, we are dying for that person.

Loyalty is a significant part of commitment in this level of relationship. In today's culture, loyalty is a lost art. We drift aimlessly from relationship to relationship, context to context, staying with it while it is easy, but rarely if ever really putting down roots to establish long-term

TIME IS A PROCESS OF DYING ONE SECOND AT A TIME. SO WHEN WE SPEND OUR TIME WITH ANOTHER PERSON, WE ARE, IN A SENSE, DYING FOR THEM.

relationships. Much of society today is living in great sadness as a result of failed relationships. Those who are coming of age today are the first generation of those who have experienced many factors that have produced relational distance and pain.

Divorce is a reality that many have experienced both as children whose parents were divorced, and now as adults who are divorced. This is changing the whole landscape of America and the concept of family. Women have joined the work force in unprecedented numbers in the past few decades, often weakening the sense of family stability. Society demands more of children; after school sports and music programs fill up more and more time, as parents try to "do the right thing" and keep their children busy with all the right advantages. More and more of these programs now take place on Sundays, which used to be seen as a day for worship and family in our culture.

And then there is entertainment: movies, video games, the Internet, the mall. All of these beckon and entice, and all too often we as believers fall into the patterns that are identical to the world. We look to have the latest name brand clothing rather than really working to be good stewards of God's money by shopping for value rather than trend or fashion. We continue to allow culture to define us, rather than realizing that as believers, we are part of a Kingdom culture than transcends prevailing culture, and is generally completely opposed to it.

In the midst of all of this, to whom and to what are you committed? Will you choose to invest yourself into fields, deep relationships with friends that produce thirty, sixty and a hundred fold harvests? Or will you decided to squander and waste your time on entertainment that evaporates the moment it's over?

The Cost of True Relationship

In the next chapter, we will explore the final court, the Holy of Holies. But before we do, I want to reflect on some concerns I have, based on various, disturbing aspects of some "Inner Court" relationships that I have observed.

In the years of ministry I have walked in, I have learned that words are cheap. Countless times, people have come to me and said things like, "Robert, God has called me to walk along side of you. The Lord has spoken to me to assist you, and I'm going to be in regular contact with you to find out how I can serve in the ministry with you." Or, "Robert, God has spoken to me to sow financially into your ministry, and I am going to be standing with you regularly."

But when the position of service the individual is offered is not glamorous, or the thrill of ministry wears off, or they realize that sowing finances into our ministry does not gain them the kind of recognition or special favor they were perhaps expecting, they quietly disappear. They are off to another ministry, another experience to thrill and entertain them. Such a "friendship" is no friendship at all.

REAL FAITHFULNESS AND COMMITMENT IS DEMONSTRATED IN WALKING FAITHFULLY WITH THE VISION AND THE PEOPLE GOD HAS LINKED YOU WITH, ESPECIALLY IN THE HARD TIMES.

What are you committed to? Who are you building life with? Who can count on you—not when it's fun and exciting, but when it's hard and boring?

Faithfulness is easy when the crowds are big, the music is moving, and life is exciting. But that is not real faithfulness; that is not real commitment. Real faithfulness and commitment is demonstrated in walking faithfully with the vision and the people God has linked you with, *especially* in the hard times, the times of pain and obscurity. This is what God is looking for; this is Kingdom perspective!

This does not mean that relationships never change, that people

NO WONDER WE HAVE AIMLESS, UNSATISFIED YOUTH— WE HAVE NOT PROVIDED THEM A SOLID COMMUNITY INTO WHICH THEY MAY GROW!

never move or that God never leads you to leave one congregation for another. I am not talking about a dysfunctional, blind loyalty that does not leave room for growth and the leadings of God in our lives.

What I *am* saying is that when those changes occur (because they will and should) there should be a level of Kingdom process and protocol observed that will confirm that it is truly the word of God leading the change, not our own whims and desires.

Because we have not adopted *Kingdom values* which lead to *Kingdom process* and *Kingdom protocol,* we are reaping the rotten fruit that comes from trying to do Kingdom work with the *systems* of Babylon (or the world's system). A perfect example of the way we use the world's systems instead of God's is reflected in the process many local churches use in hiring pastors.

In most local churches, pastors are "voted in" and "voted out"— too often moving with the whim of the congregation, the denominational leaders or the promise of a more comfortable ministry assignment. Most pastors stay for a relatively short period of time in the areas where they serve. Is this right?

Beloved, it takes *years* to build real relationships. They do not happen overnight. Trust must be established and cultivated and maintained. If the senior leader of the community of faith is moving on every four or five years, how can he or she *possibly* be deeply interacting with the believers in that congregation, let alone establishing meaningful, witnessing relationships within the community?

Youth Pastors, those whom we trust with the next generation of disciples, have an average duration of *eighteen months* at a local church. Do we expect trust, leading to accountability and true discipleship, to develop overnight? And what about the rare occasions in which it does develop quickly—what kind of price are our young people paying when their trust is broken because their leader leaves? No wonder we have aimless, unsatisfied youth—we have not provided them a solid community into which they may grow!

A Systemic Problem

And I am not blaming the youth pastors! We have a systemic problem. Many of the systems now in place of how we "do church" have not served to produce life, vitality and intergenerational anointing. We have too often mirrored the transience and rootlessness of our culture instead of doing what it really takes to impact our regions and generations through intentionally cultivating altars of long term relationships and paying the price of true commitment.

As *keepers of the flame,* our inner court relationships must move beyond superficiality. It's time for us to recognize our responsibility to honor real commitment, loyalty and steadfastness. Without paying that cost, the flame barely flickers and we are unable to go deeper or further in advancing God's Kingdom for this and future generations.

But should we dare to take the risk and embrace a willingness to pay the price, we will find that the flame not only begins to blaze intensely, but also, we will be approaching the most sacred place of all in covenant—the Holy of Holies.

CHAPTER 4

THE HOLY OF HOLIES

The Place of Covenant

We are called to be a people of covenant.

We are in covenant with God and demonstrate that by living in covenant community with one another. *Covenant must mean something.* Covenant necessarily goes beyond nice-sounding words. Covenant actually provides a solid reality upon which to build our lives. As we enter fully into God's presence in the Holy of Holies, we are called into lasting, covenant relationships with one another.

WORDS LIKE LOYALTY, SACRIFICE, RESPONSIBILITY AND SELF-DISCIPLINE ARE RARELY HEARD OR TAUGHT.

Much of the mindset of the Church today has been influenced by modern American culture, which (though a Republic) is saturated with the thought and language of democracy—a concept founded in ancient Greece. From the youngest ages these days, children talk about their "rights" and the fact that this is a free country where everyone can do as they please because we are independent. Words like loyalty, sacrifice, responsibility and self-discipline are rarely heard or taught.

Church culture has too often been determined by American culture—corporate America—where we vote in one CEO and vote out another. Shareholders have rights in the company by virtue of the stock they purchase. Too many believers feel that having their name on the membership register entitles them to rights. But friends, all of this is part of a system called democracy. Democracy may be a fine way to run a nation—but democracy is not the code of life in the Kingdom of God!

The Kingdom of God is not a democracy. We as believers have no rights; we leave them at the cross! The democratic system has its roots in Greek thought and philosophy, but we are not children of Greece; we are sons and daughters of Zion! (Zechariah 9:13).

Contracts Versus Covenant

Contracts, based on individual rights, are essentially designed to protect the individual in the event the other individual becomes an "enemy." They are based on the assumption that they will be broken, and list all the results and penalties for breaking the contract. A contract spells out how far an individual will go to assist the one to whom he is contractually bound, before a line is crossed and it really begins to cost the individual something.

Based on Greek thought, contracts are basically cheap and safe. There is a clear understanding of what you're getting into and how you can get out.

Covenants are based on family or tribal alliances, and are designed to strengthen the family or tribe and form alliances against a common enemy. They are based on the assumption that they will never be broken, even for generations. And while there are clear and drastic consequences for breaking a covenant, the expectation is that it will remain unbroken. That is why it is never entered into lightly. Rather than providing boundaries regarding how far one party will go for the other, a covenant relationship is one in which the parties are there for each other *even to their own hurt.* That is real covenant!

Covenant establishes that which lasts and cannot be broken. Covenant is not cheap. It is costly . . . indeed it costs us everything. You are pledging your life to another.

To gain a proper understanding of this most fundamental truth upon which our faith rests, let us consider the effects of covenant.

Covenant Establishes Identity

Who are we without God? For Christians today, this is a strange thing to even consider. Thousands of years after God cutting covenant with mankind, imagining life without Him is a foreign concept. If we are to understand the magnitude of God's covenant, we will need to re-visit the first time God established covenant with a man.

In our personal walk with the Lord, most of us can pinpoint the exact moment we came to Him for the first time. Just as our salvation occurred when we accepted the sacrifice of Jesus' life on the cross, God's initial contact with man also came at great price. The deep chasm separating humanity from its Creator did not always have a bridge across it.

The man Abram walked alone on this earth. Having no impartation of the Divine, he was only a man, no different from any other. After coming into covenant with the Most High God, he is changed. He is called by a new name, but not just any name. *The Lord God— Yahweh—puts His own name into Abram.* Listen for God's name (the sound of 'Yah') in these new names.

"As for me, this is my covenant with you: You will be the father of many nations. No longer will you be called Abram; your name will be Abraham, for I have made you a father of many nations . . . "

God also said to Abraham, "As for Sarai your wife, you are no longer to call her Sarai; her name will be Sarah" (Gen. 17:4-5, 15).

When God entered into covenant with man, He put His very being into Him. Just as God would one day become a man in order to save his people, in one way, He entered into humanity long before. When God established covenant with man, it cost God His name and gave us ours. When He fulfilled His covenant with man, it cost God his Son and gave us eternal life.

Covenant Brings Redemption

God's promises to man constitute our only hope for salvation. Without His unrelenting commitment to us, we could never come to know Him. And without knowing Him, we have nothing that lasts. The story of Ruth the Moabitess provides us with a powerful example of redemption coming through the phenomenon of covenant.

Ruth did not know God. Her people were pagans whom Israel was instructed to avoid. She was, as the apostle Paul would describe, *"without hope and without God in the world"* (Eph 2:12b). As such, she was destined for a life without meaning. In the years to come, no one would remember her name, and she would die knowing that her life essentially counted for nothing. Yet, by choosing to forsake her pagan ways in exchange for the ways of Israel, Ruth's legacy came to a very different end.

We all know the story. We take for granted those familiar words *"Your people will be my people and your God my God"* (Ruth 1:16b). We forget that Ruth need not have uttered them. She could have turned back like Orpah. We forget that Ruth's words *cost her something*, and that it was in speaking them that *her life was changed*. It was this choosing of covenant over contractual obligation that God chose to use to alter the course of humanity.

What comes of Ruth's uncompromising profession of covenant loyalty? The story goes on to describe God's provision for Ruth in giving her a kinsman redeemer. After Boaz marries Ruth, she bears a son. Out of the covenant, a child is born. Beyond blessing Ruth, the Gentile; Naomi, the natural-born child of God, is also blessed by this child. The woman who lost both her sons and asked that her name be changed to *bitterness* because of the Lord's harsh dealings with her, leaves this world with joy instead of sorrow.

> *The women said to Naomi: "Praise be to the LORD, who this day has not left you without a kinsman-redeemer. May he become famous throughout Israel! He will renew your life and sustain you in your old age. For your daughter-in-law, who loves you and who is better to you than seven sons, has given him birth."*
>
> *Then Naomi took the child, laid him in her lap and cared for him. The women living there said, "Naomi has a son." And they named him Obed. He was the father of Jesse, the father of David* (Ruth 4:14-17).

IN THIS BEAUTIFUL STORY OF LOYALTY, GOD'S ULTIMATE PLAN OF REDEMPTION IS REVEALED AS BLESSING BOTH JEW AND GENTILE WITH ETERNAL HOPE.

From the child that was born to Ruth, another child was born to Mary that brought redemption to the whole world. Through their covenantal relationship, Naomi and Ruth became part of something redemptive, something lasting. In this beautiful story of loyalty, God's ultimate plan of redemption is revealed as blessing both Jew and Gentile with eternal hope.

Covenant Releases Destiny

In looking back over the good things that have happened in your life, do you ever consider where they came from?

How did you first come to church?

How did you grow and change into who you are now?

Of course, the Lord has given us every good gift, but that does not negate the seed others have sown into our lives. Yes, God saved us. But we cannot forget that God chooses to work through our relationships with others as well.

Covenant relationships are those in which one party says to the other, *"No matter what, I will honor this relationship, even to my own hurt."* These are most likely the relationships in your life that have helped you reach the level of success and maturity that you have. It took someone; perhaps a teacher, a grandfather, a friend, to say, *"This one, I'm going to believe in, I'm not going to let go of until I see them released into everything God has for them."*

One such covenant relationship was that of David and Jonathan, the Shepherd and the Prince. By birth, one was bound for the throne, the other for a life of humble field work. What changed the course of their lives? A solemn vow made before God and kept in spite of opposition and threat of death was the turning point that altered the life of a Shepherd boy and turned him into a King.

> *After David had finished talking with Saul, Jonathan became one in spirit with David, and he loved him as himself. From that day Saul kept David with him and did not let him return to his father's house.*
>
> *And Jonathan **made a covenant** with David because he loved him as himself. Jonathan took off the robe he was wearing and gave it to David, along with his tunic, and even his sword, his bow and his belt* (1 Sam. 18:1-4, emphasis added).

In this symbolic act, Jonathan *bowed to the Lord's purposes* in his and David's life. Instead of insisting on his right to the throne of Israel, he laid down that call and essentially his life, so that God might have His way. *Destiny is a matter of covenant.*

Jesus, who is called the Son of David, came then from a line that would not have existed but for the covenant between Jonathan and David. The Lord shows Himself sovereign and brings glory to His name through even human relationships that honor truth, loyalty and above all, love.

By putting His name into us, God proved that He would never forsake mankind, no matter what. By grafting a Gentile into the line of the Messiah, God foreshadowed His intent to extend salvation to every nation, tribe and tongue. And by moving a Prince's heart to give his title to a Shepherd, God sealed a covenant between the two of them that would bring forth His purposes on the earth.

Enter In

With whom are you pressing into covenant relationship? Who are the handful of people you are really opening the deep places of your life to, and with whom you anticipate a life-long connection?

Obviously, your spouse and immediate family are the first sphere of this level of consecrated relationship.

But with whom else are you pressing into this sacred bond? You will find cultivating relationships the most fulfilling aspect of life. We were created for relationship with God and with one another. Covenant is what establishes this.

Consider each of the "courts" or contexts of relationship and how you can build your relationships most effectively and intentionally as you seek to live out a covenant lifestyle. Make a decision to move from "outer court" to "inner court" relationships.

Take those relationships that impact you the most and move them into the Holy of Holies. Let covenant become the lasting foundation of your relationships. As *keepers of the flame,* let us move from contract to covenant, and allow God's holy presence to seal and secure lasting relationships that will endure every test and every trial.

WHAT TO DO
WITH THE ALTARS

Then the LORD reached out his hand and touched my mouth
and said to me, "Now, I have put my words in your mouth.
See, today I appoint you over nations and kingdoms
to uproot and tear down,
to destroy and overthrow, to build and to plant".

JEREMIAH 1:9-10

As we have just learned in the previous section, not every relationship is a "Holy of Holies" relationship. In the same way that we have come to understand the God-given purpose (or level of intimacy) for each of our relationships, we will now focus on what needs to be done to each of those places in our lives.

As you read over four possibilities of how to approach your altars, take time to seek the Lord as to what He may be saying to you. In the above scripture, Jeremiah waited for the Lord to put *His* words in his mouth. He waited to hear God's instructions for each nation and kingdom that he had been appointed over.

Allow God to reveal to you what He intends for each altar of your life. Some altars need to be restored; others need to be done away with completely. In either case, when we're certain that we've heard His voice clearly, we can deal with our altars confidently, knowing that our work is not in vain.

CHAPTER 5

BUILDING THE ALTARS

The Call to Relational Integrity

Dr. Dan Juster, one of the leading spiritual thinkers of our time, has a beautiful family. One night, in Beersheva, Israel, his daughter Simcha had dinner with my wife and me.

Simcha shared, "Our whole life, my brothers and sister and I were trained by our father never to ask 'What church do you go to?' but rather 'What community of faith are you a part of?' He drilled it into us over and over again that the Church was not a building or set of programs that you could pick and choose from. Rather, it is a set of living relationships that you give yourself to for better or worse, and you don't leave those relationships any more than you would leave your family. The Church is a lifelong community."

Oh that more fathers and mothers would be teaching their children the importance of relationships, and the value of loyalty and community!

What is Your Community of Faith?

I remember one evening when my wife and I visited with a couple we had recently come to know. We had met the husband a few times, and this was the first time we were meeting his wife. They were believers, businesspeople in their community, and attended the largest church in their city.

ATTENDING A MEETING ONE OR TWO DAYS A WEEK, GENERALLY WHERE ONE PERSON SPEAKS AND EVERYONE ELSE LISTENS, DOES VERY LITTLE TO FACILITATE CHRISTIAN COMMUNITY.

Over the course of our dinner, they began to share some of the struggles they were going through in their marriage and extended family relationships. My wife and I simply listened and provided a loving and supportive atmosphere for them as they began to share. Soon, the wife was crying and really unburdening her heart. We prayed with them and they expressed their gratitude for the time we had together.

Then, as we were leaving, they said something that amazed us.

"Thanks so much for listening and sharing with us," they said. "We really don't have anyone we can talk to."

"What about your church?" my wife asked, wanting them to get some follow up support. "Aren't you close with people there?"

"No, we really don't have any close friends there," they replied, "the relationships and atmosphere of the church is more social."

"How long have you attended there?" I asked.

"Twenty years," came the reply.

So, what community of faith are YOU a part of? I am not asking what building you attend on Sunday morning. That may or may not be your community. Attending a meeting one or two days a week, generally where one person speaks and everyone else listens, does very little to facilitate Christian community. So, if your fellowship is not actively providing an "on ramp" to meaningful relationships for you, then it is your responsibility to begin reaching out and seeking to establish those relationships.

Invite some people over to your home for a night of fellowship. Include prayer and testimony time in that evening. Instead of going out to a movie, take time to learn the story of each others lives, and what God is doing in your midst. Make some humble, deliberate decisions to take off masks of Christian perfection, and admit weaknesses and struggles.

It doesn't take many—just a few people walking together in community can bring forth a lot of life!

Here are some practical ways to build the altars of relationship in your local community of faith:

- Take time after service to fellowship with people. You may even go out to a meal or for a social time together.
- Become a part of a small group—cell group, life group, Sunday school class or equipping course.
- Get involved in a ministry in which you can serve Christ with others as you care for children in the nursery, evangelize in the neighborhood, practice on the praise and worship team, etc.
- Invite others in the fellowship to your home or to attend edifying events with you.

We have seen a good increase of community-building initiatives within evangelical Christianity in the past few decades, and this is encouraging. For example, Promise Keepers has been extremely successful in launching men's prayer and accountability groups. This is certainly a good step in the right direction.

However, we must be careful to make sure that we are experiencing relationship in an *authentic* way, and not just in theory. Saying, "Our church has started some fellowship groups" is different from

FELLOWSHIP AND RELATIONSHIPS CANNOT BE SOME-THING WE DO AS AN OPTION; IT MUST BE SOMETHING WE ARE BY DEFINITION AND PRIORITY.

realizing, "The Church IS a Fellowship group." Fellowship and relationships cannot be something we DO as an option; it must be something we ARE by definition and priority.

Don't be surprised if this is not easy! The enemy resists true Christian relationship with all his might! This is why he specializes in offense, division, hurt, rejection, gossip, etc. He knows that one can put a thousand to flight and two can put ten thousand. The forces of evil know the power of Kingdom unity and will do everything within their power to thwart that virtue!

The Enemy Attacks Healthy Relationships

Just as when we are attacked for pursuing right relationships, Nehemiah and his workers were mocked and reviled when they resolved to heed the Lord's command to rebuild the wall. When faced with opposition and discouragement, the workers had to choose whether to give in to this or continue in the difficult work that rebuilding broken things always is.

Hear the cry of Nehemiah as he chose to honor the Lord's call to press on for the sake of what is truly important; building a strong foundation that upholds godly relationships.

> *After I looked things over, I stood up and said to the nobles, the officials and the rest of the people, "Don't be afraid of them. Remember the Lord, who is great and awesome, and **fight for your brothers, your sons and your daughters, your wives and your homes**"* (Neh. 4:14, emphasis added).

So, we are called to fight for our relationships. Remember that our relationships are attacked by the enemy in a myriad of subtle ways. From past hurts and grievances that remain unforgiven and unforgotten in our hearts, to fear and mistrust about the future; he will use anything and everything to keep us from walking in one accord.

Whatever keeps you distanced from others by attacking your relationships, will dampen the coals of love and caring and cause your love for your brothers and sisters in the community of faith to wax cold. Decide now to mend those altars and tend the flame.

It is time to BUILD THE ALTARS! It is time to press through to real, radical, balanced, authentic Christianity. It is time to say no to the prevailing Greek-based culture of self, individuality, consumerism and "me" focus; and arise to the call to Zion! As *keepers of the flame*, we are called to live for God, for our families and for the family of families that is the Kingdom of God!

CHAPTER 6

REPAIRING THE ALTARS

The Call to Freedom

The fallen state of this world constantly wears on the relational fabric of our lives. Rebellion, rejection, broken families and misunderstandings erode and dismantle our relational altars. All of us have relationships that have suffered from one problem or another, and about which we feel a great deal of pain and sadness.

The healing of these relationships is not important only because of the emotional pain or disappointment we feel from their breakdown. Healing is important because relationships are God's pipeline for His purposes. Relationships are the arteries, blood vessels and capillaries through which the Life of God flows and reaches out to the whole Body.

When we allow relationships to break down through the sin of division, we are hindering God's ability to pour out His abundant Life through His Body. So Paul writes, *"From him the whole body, joined and held together by every supporting ligament, grows and builds itself up in love, as each part does its work"* (Eph. 4:16).

A Solid Foundation

For many, the relational altars that need to be repaired are some of the earliest and most basic relationships in life—family relationships of parents, children, brothers and sisters, extended family. Some of your family may not be believers. Some may not even be alive. There may be painful memories that until today are keeping you from freely giving and receiving the grace of God in the deepest way possible.

HEALING IS IMPORTANT BECAUSE RELATIONSHIPS ARE GOD'S PIPELINE FOR HIS PURPOSES.

Revisit these altars. See what has broken down and what you can do to repair it. This does not mean that every relationship will be healed and perfected. Relationship requires both parties to walk together. But it *does* mean that you will move into blessing as you endeavor, as much as possible, to walk in love, forgiveness and right relationship with your family members—even those who may have hurt you terribly.

I fully believe that the Lord can bring great restoration through the inner healing of prayer even to relationship issues with those who have died. Ask the Lord to bring you to a deep place in your heart, and pray through these wounds or places of unforgiveness with Him, giving forgiveness where needed, and receiving forgiveness from the Lord where you have been wrong.

Mending Fallen Bridges

It is not only family altars that need to be repaired, but other meaningful relationships that have been broken.

As a young boy, our family was extremely involved with the church we attended. The senior pastor of that church was always very kind and encouraging to me, and had a way of affirming my calling, even though I was very young; eleven or twelve at the time.

At some point, my parents got involved in a doctrinal dispute with him and the other leaders of the church, so we left the fellowship which had really nurtured me and been truly influential in my relationship with Christ.

Years later, as a freshman in Bible college, I realized how much of my understanding of Christ and the Church had been formed by the faithfulness of this pastor, and what a profound influence and example he had been in my life. Though I had not spoken with him in years and my parent's leaving that church had been difficult, I wrote him a letter thanking him for his faithfulness to the Lord's calling on his life and told him that I was now entering ministry. I shared with him that his planting in my life was still bearing fruit, even in fields beyond his immediate knowledge.

I received a beautiful letter back from him, thanking me for what I had expressed. In some small way, I think my letter was also a healing for him from the hurt of having our family leave the church after he had pastored them for many years.

Restoration through Humility

There are many ways we can rebuild altars that have broken down. This does not mean that we chain ourselves to the past or look for things that have changed to go back to the way they once were. That is unrealistic and unhealthy. It *does* mean that, as much as possible, we take an honest account of the relational interactions in our lives that have been burdensome or hurtful, and seek forgiveness for those times we have been wrong and extend forgiveness when we have been wronged.

Those who seek God's will for their lives are commanded to honor the relationships in their lives by seeking to replace injury with pardon, and enmity with love.

One of, if not *the* most damaged relationship in the Bible is that of Jacob and Esau. From the womb they contended for blessing, and lived in strife for want of it. After Jacob receives his Father's blessing and the blessing of God, he is still not fulfilled. The Lord requires that he acknowledge his wrongdoing to his brother and seek to make things between them right. Despite great fear over the wrath of Esau, Jacob obeys the Lord and risks losing everything he has worked to achieve, that he might be at peace with his brother.

> *But Esau ran to meet Jacob and embraced him; he threw his arms around his neck and kissed him. And they wept . . . "No, please!" said Jacob. "If I have found favor in your eyes, accept this gift from me. For to see your face is like seeing the face of God, now that you have received me favorably. Please accept the present that was brought to you, for God has been gracious to me and I have all I need." And because Jacob insisted, Esau accepted it* (Gen. 33:4, 10-11).

The reason Jacob gives for being able to extend his hand to Esau is the Lord's graciousness. When those who are in opposition become more focused on God's grace than on their own sense of right and wrong, they are no longer bound to, but freed from the past.

Perhaps the most poignant example of reconciliation given in Scripture is the exchange between Jesus and Peter after the resurrection.

Peter was a man of extremes, acting on his impulses immediately, often without considering the consequences of being wrong. Because of his great faith, Peter was afforded some of the most memorable experiences Christ had with his disciples. Whether he was right or wrong in his convictions, the Lord recognized that Peter's heart was steadfast and was therefore willing to reconcile their relationship.

When Jesus tells Peter that he will deny Him three times before the cock crows, Peter tells him that he will never turn his back on Him. After denying his Lord, I'm sure Peter could not imagine any consolation able to ease the grief He felt. He must have known a sorrow over sin that most of us may never experience. How does Jesus respond to Peter's betrayal? With harsh words and angry contempt?

In the following passage, notice the number of times Jesus asks Peter his question. And remember, when the Lord desires to restore the shattered places between us, His justice is as righteous as it is poetic.

WHEN THOSE WHO ARE IN OPPOSITION BECOME MORE FOCUSED ON GOD'S GRACE THAN ON THEIR OWN SENSE OF RIGHT AND WRONG, THEY ARE NO LONGER BOUND TO, BUT FREED FROM THE PAST.

> *When they had finished eating, Jesus said to Simon Peter, "Simon son of John, do you truly love me more than these?"*
>
> *"Yes, Lord," he said, "you know that I love you."*
>
> *Jesus said, "Feed my lambs."*
>
> *Again Jesus said, "Simon son of John, do you truly love me?"*
>
> *He answered, "Yes, Lord, you know that I love you."*
>
> *Jesus said, "Take care of my sheep."*
>
> *The third time he said to him, "Simon son of John, do you love me?"*
>
> *Peter was hurt because Jesus asked him the third time, "Do you love me?" He said, "Lord, you know all things; you know that I love you."*
>
> *Jesus said, "Feed my sheep"* (John 21:15-18a).

Notice that the first two times Jesus asked if Peter loved Him, Jesus used the verb *agapao* which refers to unconditional love. However, Peter only responds with *phileo* which refers to brotherly love. In other words, Peter can't meet Jesus where He is. However, the third time, Jesus asked Peter for love using the word *phileo*. Jesus was willing to meet Peter where Peter was. Relationships are restored when we meet people where they are instead of trying to get them to be where we expect them to be.

Is there a broken altar in your life? Are you willing to humble yourself and meet that person where they are? Will you sacrifice your own expectations for the sake of keeping the flame alive on the altar of relationship?

We Need One Another!

With Christ as our example, we have no excuse for letting godly relationships fall by the wayside. God has chosen to make us interdependent; we need one another.

So, relationships are worth the time and effort they take to maintain. One principle to note here is: The relationship is almost always more important than being right.

RELATIONSHIPS ARE RESTORED WHEN WE MEET PEOPLE WHERE THEY ARE INSTEAD OF TRYING TO GET THEM TO BE WHERE WE EXPECT THEM TO BE.

How often have you so insisted on being "right" and winning an argument or dispute that you lost the relationship? Standing firm for righteousness is necessary. But too often we fail to speak the truth in love. We use the truth as a sword to destroy others instead of as a liberating force that sets them (and us) free from the past.

Recognizing that the purposes of God are fulfilled through our relationships with others, we must always seek to forgive and move forward into the will of God.

CHAPTER 7

STRENGTHENING THE ALTARS
The Call to Intentional Lifestyles

The Law of Entropy is just as true regarding relationships as it is anything else.

According to the natural order of things, if objects are left alone, they will break down. In order for our relationships to stay strong and vital, in order for our altars to be in good working order, they need to be regularly maintained and strengthened.

Strengthening the relationships in our life, especially strengthening them in a Kingdom way, takes not only effort and discipline, but also investment. The bottom line is that there are really only two things you and I have to invest in this earth. Time and money.

I know it may sound very carnal to talk about spiritual things in earthy terms like time and money, but God doesn't seem to think these things are carnal! For example, what was one of His Commandments, by which the children of Israel were to affirm and strengthen their covenant with Him?

Remember the Sabbath; Keep It Holy!

In other words, God said, "I want one day out of seven set aside for me. This is your day to think about me, remember me, love me, teach

your children of me. This day is mine. It is our investment in each other." In other words, God valued time spent in relationship with Him.

THE BOTTOM LINE IS THAT THERE ARE REALLY ONLY TWO THINGS YOU AND I HAVE TO INVEST IN THIS EARTH. TIME AND MONEY.

When we realize the historic power of the Sabbath, we see that it is this honoring of God with their time that has kept the Jewish community together as a people for thousands of years. You are most likely familiar with the adage, "The Jews did not make the Sabbath; the Sabbath made the Jews." In other words, the results of honoring this day were so powerful that they literally defined and kept the Jewish people from the sea of assimilation in culture after culture, generation after generation.

A primary way to strengthen relationships is through the investment of time. It is setting aside valuable time to spend with people so that the relationship grows and matures in powerful and dynamic ways.

Spend Quality Time Together

But please hear and understand that phrase "quality time." If we are to have real results from our investment, it must be an INTENTIONAL investment understood by both parties. This is why altars of relationship must be built with common goals and understandings before they can be strengthened.

What do I mean? I am saying that simply spending time together does not guarantee that a relationship is growing; that time needs to have a focus and sense of purpose, or it can be wasted. In the same way that God did not just say, "Remember the Sabbath", but said, "Remember the Sabbath and KEEP IT HOLY"; both parties must come into shared time with a sense of purpose and a realization of the preciousness of that time.

For example, as I travel around the country, I am often invited to attend Pastors' Fellowship meetings from time to time in different cities. These are usually informal meetings in which area ministers get together once a week or once a month for prayer and fellowship.

At times, I come into these meetings, and within a few minutes it is clear that there is very little *strengthening of the altars* going on.

Conversation is shallow

People don't really seem to know one another.

There is little direction in the meeting.

*It generally feels like we are simply passing the time
and "punching the time clock" of doing our duty by being seen
at a function we are expected to attend.*

But other times when I walk into these meetings, there is a totally different atmosphere.

There is a sense of purpose.

*People introduce themselves to one another
and take time to ask questions about each others families,
not just each others ministries.*

A real openness of sharing exists in the meeting.

Time in prayer together is easy, deep and rich.
This is koinonia.

Koinonia (koy-nohn-ee-ah) is a Greek word used throughout the New Testament to describe the special bond that exists between believers as they unite in the common goal of furthering the Gospel. This intimate fellowship, or close brotherhood, is made possible only by the Holy Spirit. This is the Psalm 133 blessing in which God commands a corporate blessing on those who dwell together in unity!

Invest in Relationships

The other investment we make is the investment of our resources; our finances. It is easy to say we have a burden for something—we believe in it—but are we willing to give of our storehouse to strengthen the altar we are believing for?

WE SAY WE CAN'T AFFORD IT, BUT WHAT WE REALLY MEAN IS THAT WE CAN'T AFFORD IT WITHOUT A SACRIFICE.

I think of a precious couple who are part of the staff here at Eagles Wings. Don and Joanne are in their early sixties. At a time when many people are content to retire and relax, they came into contact with Eagles' Wings and the values and vision we carry.

They began volunteering their time at different conferences. They were faithful in their volunteering, even when it was hard. They proved they were not "fair weather friends." Then they really felt God stirring them to give more of themselves, but they had given so much already—what could they do?

Many of us would have said, "Well, I am being faithful in my volunteering, and I give what I can," never realizing that the "what I can" statement we are making is more accurately said, "I am giving what I can *without it really costing me anything.*" Most of us could give *much* more than we do—both in terms of time and money—but we are unwilling to allow our giving to affect our lifestyle! We say we can't afford it, but what we really mean is that we can't afford it without a sacrifice.

But Don and Joanne are not these kind of people. They were being intentional about strengthening the relational altar that they have with the Eagles' Wings community because they saw us as good ground that would produce good fruit. Don and Joanne made *lifestyle changes,* so that they were no longer serving their American, middle class lifestyle, but their lifestyle was serving the Kingdom.

They sold their home, which they had lived in for twenty-five years and moved into a much smaller townhouse, which required much less of their care and attention, so that they had more free time. They sold their big car for a less expensive model. Step by step, they made *choices* that allowed them to be available to God's purposes that were in the altar of Eagles' Wings. They strengthened that altar in their life.

Now Don and Joanne are full-time missionaries with Eagles' Wings. They have helped lead missions teams to Honduras and Israel. They're a part of our conference staff and are also active in our ministry base in New York City. They are flowing in the relationships and purposes around those relationships they hoped for, but they are there because they made intentional choices about their lifestyle that strengthened the altars in their life.

Take up your Cross

Beloved, it strikes me that we have heard so much about the finished work of the cross, and heard so many times that "Jesus paid it all," we no longer consider the COST of biblical Christianity.

If we want to see powerful, societal impact in our day . . .

if we want to move out of religious irrelevance into spiritual impact, we must pay the price.

We have to make lifestyle choices about the kind of lives we are going to live as believers, and we need to invest ourselves into Kingdom fields that are producing fruit that remains.

CHAPTER 8

TEARING DOWN THE ALTARS
The Call to Spiritual Boldness

Finally, we need to look at which altars exist in our lives that are not dedicated to the Lord, but are actually allowing the forces of the enemy to continue to operate in our lives.

We cannot excuse, justify or comply with them.

We must attack them with the same zeal and fervent spirit that the reformers of Israel who tore down false idols throughout their history did.

Shatter Inner, Unholy Vows

Many of us, unconsciously, have at some point in our lives made inner vows, or oaths, that have affected our subconscious thought patterns and the decisions that result from those thought patterns. It takes a great deal of prayer, inner honesty, discipline and perseverance to gain an objective look at ourselves and to honestly look at what thought patterns we have that are not healthy. Once found, we must trace those patterns to their roots and deal with them. Usually, these negative inner vows are a result of hurt, disappointment, rejection or betrayal. We go through a painful experience and we say that we "learn from it," when, in reality, too many times what we really mean is that we are going to shut down our desire to trust and be vulnerable.

EVENTUALLY, OVER TIME, THESE THOUGHT PATTERNS BECOME SO EMBEDDED IN US THAT WE ACCEPT THEM AS PART OF OUR PERSONALITY.

These areas of unconscious darkness are where the enemy loves to dwell. Eventually, over time, these thought patterns become so embedded in us that we accept them as part of our personality. We "own" them, even though they are not really us, and they are not healthy or godly.

God calls us to live in a climate of love. Love believes all things, hopes, endures, and keeps no record of wrongs. But from the very beginning, the enemy seeks to inject the poison of hurt and disappointment into our lives, in order to keep this love as some kind of unreachable ideal, rather than the foundational reality of our walk with the Lord.

I remember one individual who joined the Eagles' Wings several years ago. She had a strong sense of calling to our ministry, and really knew the Lord had called her to be with us. Yet, there was some kind of emotional wall around her heart, keeping her from really opening up and entering into a trusting relationship with our community, and especially with Ana and me.

This went on for months. Consistently, Ana and I reached out to her and sought to affirm her, letting her know of our unconditional love for her and our belief in God's purpose for her life. While her responses were always appreciative, they were always surface and there was never a feeling of comfort or ease in the relationship.

Finally, Ana and I confronted her about this sense of isolation we felt from her. Initially, she denied it. Weeks went by and we confronted her again. Finally, she admitted it was there, but said she had no idea why, and that though she knew beyond a shadow of a doubt that God had called her to the Eagles' Wings community, that she felt a huge wall around her, keeping her from entering in to real community, especially with Ana and me.

Time went on and we again approached her regarding the situation. Finally, one night, through the help of the Holy Spirit, gentle questioning, seeking for honesty and an atmosphere of love; she shared a story from her past.

Many years before, her father had served for years under a senior pastor in ministry, but had been very hurt and wounded by that leader, and had left the ministry. From that point on, she said, though her family had always attended church, the decision at home was that they were never again going to open up to "church people" deeply—especially leaders.

Though she had no idea that she had absorbed this offense and made it her own, and though consciously she was not aware that this inner vow of her parents had been passed on to her, we realized we had found the root. We encouraged her to take the authority that was hers in Christ to tear down this false altar in her soul's territory that was still a power center for the enemy.

A glorious freedom came in that moment, and in an instant there was a great breakthrough in her life—in her interactions and relationships with us and the whole community. She began to see breakthrough in many areas around her, as she walked into the freedom of trusting the family of believers God had called her to walk with. There was truly a night and day change in her as she was freed from the enemy's power that was operating from the "old altar".

It takes great courage and discipline to tear down old altars—to think deeply about your life, to evaluate what you say and do—and more importantly *why* you say and do it. **Tearing down false altars takes steadfast gazing into the light of the Word of God, continual inner love and desire for truth, as well as a commitment to a community that will speak the truth to one another in love.** It also takes "loving not your life unto death". In this sense, it is the death that we face every day as we are delivered from the "old man" into the fullness of the life of Messiah.

Breaking the Fear of Man

Each of us desires to be liked. Almost everyone has a desire to be thought well of, respected and heard. Innately, we are conditioned to be a part of the "in crowd." This is because God has designed us to function optimally in community.

> THERE IS A HUGE DIFFERENCE BETWEEN ENJOYING RELATIONSHIPS AS A BLESSING IN OUR LIFE, AND NEEDING THE AFFIRMATION OF OTHERS TO BE SECURE IN OUR IDENTITY.

But there is a huge difference between *enjoying* relationships as a blessing in our life, and *needing* the affirmation of others to be secure in our identity. Our identity, our security in whose we are, should come from our walk with our Father and His ever-affirming love for us.

Human relationships should be a blessing, but not the foundation of our being. The foundation and cornerstone of our self-image should be our love relationship with God.

Because many of us are unwilling to pay the price to live in deep honesty with ourselves and root out our insecurities, we are often bound to our sense of other people's opinions of us. When this unhealthy need is manifested in the Church and coupled with the dynamic of leaders who represent God in some way, it can produce a very unhealthy "church" system based on leaders taking advantage of people's weaknesses and need for affirmation and inner security.

Unhealthy leaders seek to control, dominate, intimidate and manipulate. If leaders are not healthy, they can easily move into patterns of control and manipulation which are laced with all kinds of flattery and nice-sounding words that are really just used to keep people "under control."

This can produce a co-dependent system that easily masks itself in all kinds of spiritual-sounding language. Congregants can accuse leaders of being manipulative and controlling; leaders can accuse congregants of being rebellious or having a "Jezebel spirit."

Moving in Corporate Anointing

The reality is that we must *all* be willing to face our faults and shortcomings honestly, move into the mutual and objective accountability Scripture calls for, (and I believe God calls leaders to have *greater* levels of true, outside accountability, not lesser) and be committed to one another even in the midst of our faults. Division is sin and is not what God is looking for! If we do not grow into this understanding, we will be moving in accusation rather than reconciliation, which will breed still more division rather than the unity the Lord desires.

If the Church as we know it is to move into her destiny—which is to be in unity, without spot or wrinkle—then we must begin to attack the spirit of the fear of man from both ends. Leaders must not seek to inappropriately control people through taking advantage of their insecurities and weaknesses; and the Church as a whole must seek to find our emotional wholeness from a loving relationship with God first, and affirmation and relationship with others, second.

Let us have the boldness and courage to tear down false altars (those places where we have empowered the enemy consciously or even sub-consciously) and determine that we will walk in the fear of the Lord, not the fear of man. Then we will be able to speak the truth in love, with all humility, out of a teachable heart, in the context of mutual submission and genuine, plural accountability. This will begin to produce the Kingdom culture that will change the world.

THE SACRIFICE

Therefore, I urge you, brothers, in view of God's mercy,
to offer your bodies as living sacrifices,
holy and pleasing to God—
this is your spiritual act of worship.
Do not conform any longer to the pattern of this world,
but be transformed by the renewing of your mind.
Then you will be able to test and approve what God's will is—
his good, pleasing and perfect will.

ROMANS 12:1-2

W hat is a sacrifice?

Scripture is full of sacrifices. From beginning to end, the Bible tells story after story about sacrifices.

Abel offered an acceptable sacrifice. Cain's was unacceptable. Isaac was placed on the altar as a sacrifice. Jesus hung as a sacrifice on the cross. Paul calls us to offer our bodies as living sacrifices.

So if our altars are built and our relationships in good order, then what must go on the altar as our sacrifice and offering unto the Lord?

In this second section of our journey together, we will explore the acceptable sacrifices of the heart which you and I, as *keepers of the flame,* must continually offer up to the Lord.

The Sacrifice *Then*

As *the substance* of worship, the sacrifice served as the meat, or the offering rendered to the Lord. It was the thing; the valuable, precious thing, which had to be given over completely to the Lord. God made it very clear that the sacrifice laid on the altar was to be perfect; one without blemish. Consider this description in the priestly code:

> *You must present a male without defect from the cattle, sheep or goats in order that it may be accepted on your behalf. Do not bring anything with a defect, because it will not be accepted on your behalf. When anyone brings from the herd or flock a fellowship offering to the LORD to fulfill a special vow or as a freewill offering, it must be without defect or blemish to be acceptable* (Lev. 22:19-21).

Indeed, Scripture records the very real possibility that all offerings are *not* accepted, and that there is potential tragedy for those who offered inappropriate sacrifices.

> *Now Abel kept flocks, and Cain worked the soil. In the course of time Cain brought some of the fruits of the soil as an offering to the LORD. But Abel brought fat portions from some of the firstborn of his flock. The LORD looked with favor on Abel and his offering, but on Cain and his offering he did not look with favor. So Cain was very angry, and his face was downcast. Then the LORD said to Cain, "Why are you angry? Why is your face downcast? If you do what is right, will you not be accepted?"* (Gen. 4:2-7a).

The concept and act of sacrifice was foundational in Jewish culture. There were many occasions to bring sacrifices to the Temple. Coming into the presence of God without the right sacrifice brought in the right way would have been unthinkable.

The Sacrifice *Now: Thoughts for Today*

We can apply the sacrifice in our own lives to the condition of our hearts and the work of our hands. Contrary to the "God accepts you just as you are" mentality of today, in order for what we offer up to the Lord to mean something to him, it must meet His requirements of purity and diligence. God exhorts us to bring not *a* sacrifice but *an acceptable* sacrifice. And that is a sacrifice which costs us something.

WE ARE NOT TO BE THE SAME TODAY AS WE WERE YESTERDAY. WE ARE BEING TRANSFORMED FROM GLORY TO GLORY.

King David said, *"I will not sacrifice to the Lord my God burnt offerings that cost me nothing"* (2 Sam. 24:24a). All too often today, we bring the Lord cheap sacrifices. We offer words of songs, but our hearts are hard and unyielding. We write out checks, but are unwilling to give our time and our energy.

Yet Scripture is full of admonitions that call us to demonstrate the *reality* of our salvation by the *lives* we live. Again and again, we are reminded that salvation is not a subjective condition, but a dynamic process that involves everything we are and everything we do.

> *But someone will say, "You have faith; I have deeds." Show me your faith without deeds, and I will show you my faith by what I do. You believe that there is one God. Good! Even the demons believe that—and shudder. You foolish man, do you want evidence that faith without deeds is useless? Was not our ancestor Abraham considered righteous for what he did when he offered his son Isaac on the altar? You see that his faith and his actions were working together, and his faith was made complete by what he did. And the scripture was fulfilled that says, "Abraham*

believed God, and it was credited to him as righteousness," and
he was called God's friend. You see that a person is justified by
what he does and not by faith alone (James 2:18-24).

Acceptable worship involves daily sacrifice. Putting ourselves on the altar
demands righteous and holy living rooted in obedience and motivated out of a pure heart.

While it is true that God receives everyone just as he is, the process
of sanctification (which follows justification by faith) mandates a process
of maturing, purifying and growing spiritually. Entering His presence in
worship constantly changes us. We are not to be the same today as we
were yesterday. We are being transformed from glory to glory.

What's acceptable in worship is not what I *am* but what I *am*
becoming! *"Therefore, if anyone is in Christ, he is a new creation; old things*
have passed away; behold, all things have become new" (2 Cor. 5:17
NKJV). What Paul is conveying here in the original Greek is the concept of rebirth; of real, new, eternal life. "I *have become* a new creation.
I *am becoming* more and more like Christ; and I *will be* like Him!"

The Heart Sacrifice

The sacrifices of God are a broken spirit;
a broken and contrite heart,
O God, you will not despise
(Psalm 51:17).

Every sacrifice begins with the heart. For the Hebrew, the heart
(*lev*) is the inner person. The heart isn't just a caldron of emotions and
sentiments and irrational reactions. Rather, the heart is the true, inner
self that builds an altar of worship to God.

Much in our culture today tells us to "follow our hearts." We are
encouraged to listen to our heart and follow what "feels right."

God knows what is in our hearts; those things hidden from natural observation. He sees that our hearts can be filled with sinful thoughts and feelings. The light of His truth must expose our hearts, our inner selves. Jeremiah 17:9 declares, *"The heart is deceitful above all things and beyond cure. Who can understand it?"*

As we look at the heroes of faith in Scripture, we see that time and time again, the sacrifices they offered to the Lord were not those that necessarily seemed in their best interests. Had they been intent on responding to the feelings of their hearts instead of using their inner passion to uphold the purposes of God; we would not be referring to them as the heroes of our faith. These saints realized that the Kingdom of God operates on a very different value system.

HAD THEY BEEN INTENT ON RESPONDING TO THE FEELINGS OF THEIR HEARTS INSTEAD OF USING THEIR INNER PASSION TO UPHOLD THE PURPOSES OF GOD; WE WOULD NOT BE REFERRING TO THEM AS THE HEROES OF OUR FAITH.

As we study these sacrifices, deeply consider not only the sacrifice, but also *the relationships surrounding the sacrifice,* which made up the altar, or context, of the offering. Each sacrifice must be accompanied by a broken and contrite heart, an attitude of repentance and a humility acknowledging that the sacrifice is not a demand on God.

Remember . . .

My sacrifice doesn't obligate God to speak or act in a certain way.

My sacrifice doesn't earn me a special hearing before God's throne.

My sacrifice isn't on display for others to esteem or honor me.

The sacrifice is never brought with an expectation to get something in return. Rather, *keepers of the flame* bring sacrifices and offerings as acts of worship and praise to the Lord for the sacrifice He became for them.

In the coming chapters, we will examine what some of these key sacrifices are. Let's begin by considering the legacy of Abraham—the father of our faith, whose heartfelt sacrifice paved the way for every sacrifice to come.

The Sacrifice of the Most Precious

All his life, Abraham longed for a son, an heir. With a broken heart, he cried out to God. For without an heir, all his possessions and inheritance would go only to a servant in his household.

Of course, the miraculous story of God's provision of a son to Abraham and Sarah is well-known. Far advanced in years and seemingly beyond the ability of God to provide, a miracle happened.

Inexpressible joy was theirs.

Isaac was born.

Imagine Abraham's overwhelming grief and confusion when the Lord commands him to offer his beloved son, Isaac, as a sacrifice. Even if this story is so familiar to us, let's pause for a moment and consider its full impact.

WHAT'S MOST DIFFICULT FOR THE BELIEVER IS PUTTING A GOD-GIVEN DREAM, VISION OR WORD ON THE ALTAR.

It's not that the human sacrifice of Isaac was the dramatic part. In Abraham's time and culture, human sacrifice was not uncommon, especially the sacrifice of the first born. What today seems horrific and barbaric to us was somewhat commonplace and understood in the cultures surrounding Abraham in that day.

The dramatic and heart-wrenching aspect of the story commands our attention. Abraham is called on to offer what's most precious and dear to him. *He must place on the altar the very realization of God's promises in his life!*

Abraham's promises, hopes and dreams—given by God Himself, must be laid down as a sacrifice upon the altar.

Imagine such a command from God given to you. For a moment, remember back to your time of salvation. Certainly surrendering one's life to God as an unbeliever was not as difficult as what Abraham was asked to do!

In confessing Jesus as Lord, we exchanged existence for life; darkness for light; despair for hope; sickness for health; guilt for forgiveness; impurity for holiness. What a wonderful sacrifice to offer our lost and dead selves for a life forever with Jesus! It seemed hard at the time, but what a joyful sacrifice it became.

As we matured in Christ—dying in our souls to various destructive habits, strongholds and sinful attitudes—we experienced momentary sorrow and pain. The end result, however, was ever-increasing breakthroughs filled with new revelation and wisdom in our spiritual walks.

But what's most difficult for the believer is putting a God-given dream, vision or word on the altar. We know that its origin isn't flesh, but Spirit. We stand firm and confident that God who is faithful will complete the work that He started in us. So what happens in us when God's next word to us seems to contradict His last? When what He promised, He then asks to be put on the altar?

To Sacrifice that which is Most Dear

God promised a son, an heir out of whom would come a people who would bless the nations. Now God commands, "Sacrifice the son. Kill the promise!" I find it fascinating that Abraham did not rationalize away God's command.

Abraham didn't say, "Well, these just must be my own thoughts."

Abraham didn't "rebuke the devil," reasoning that the enemy had come to "steal from him."

Instead, Abraham recognized the voice of God. He heard and understood that God was asking him to do a very, very difficult thing: *to lay down that which was most precious.*

What is most precious to you?

Is it a relationship?

Your house?

Your ministry?

Your reputation?

Your future?

How Will You Respond?

If we really want to bring an acceptable sacrifice—a sacrifice of praise —the real possibility exists that at some moment in our relationship with God, He will speak to us in the same way He spoke to Abraham. God will ask us to place that which is *most precious* to us on the altar.

We will probably be tempted, as I am sure Abraham must have been, to rationalize the sacrifice away, rebuke it or even ignore it.

But if we, like Abraham, choose to obey and believe God, some-thing awesome will happen in our relationship with God.

If we will to believe that God asks for things with a purpose, and that purpose always includes our *greatest good,* then we will move into the *supernatural faith* and *spiritual authority* that Abraham possessed.

Too often we want *supernatural faith*—the gift of faith—without the cost of sacrifice.

Too often we desire *spiritual authority*—the authority to move in the realm of the miraculous—without first bringing to the altar what is *most precious* to us.

When we commit our most precious treasures to the Lord, we will begin to see greater freedom and experience inexpressible joy beyond our wildest dreams. For the Lord takes what is most precious to us and uses it far beyond anything we could do or imagine.

Never Own Anything

Years ago, A.W. Tozer wrote a now out-of-print pamphlet entitled, *Five Spiritual Vows.* He convincingly penned these spiritual mandates for mature Christians:

1. Deal thoroughly with sin.
2. Never pass on anything about anyone that would harm them.
3. Never own anything.
4. Never accept glory.
5. Never defend yourself.

The one that applies to us at this point is, "Never own anything." Whatever we possess possesses us. Think of how much time and energy our possessions demand of us in maintenance, repairs and replacement. Too often, we value ourselves and others by what we have instead of whose we are. We call the blessings of God the stuff that we accumulate instead of the relationship with God out of which the provisions flow.

> WHEN WE COMMIT OUR MOST PRECIOUS TREASURES TO THE LORD, WE WILL BEGIN TO SEE GREATER FREEDOM AND EXPERIENCE INEXPRESSIBLE JOY BEYOND OUR WILDEST DREAMS.

We buy insurance, install security systems, rent storage units and employ people or pay institutions to protect and house our stuff. We grieve when something we possess is broken or stolen. We forget the Giver and too often simply focus on the gifts.

The Lord Has Need of It

"And if anyone says to you, 'Why are you doing this?' say, 'The Lord has need of it,' and immediately he will send it here" (Mark 11:3 NKJV).

Yes, we guard and protect that which is most precious to us not to own or possess but to steward it for that *kairos* moment when we hear, *"The Lord has need of it."*

The most precious things in life are to be held very, very lightly, not to be grasped in demanding ownership, but treasured in reverent stewardship.

That includes both things and relationships.

Our most precious things, *your* most precious things, are not yours. They belong to Him.

Is *that which is most precious to you* on the altar?

CHAPTER 9

STANDING FIRM
The Sacrifice of Unswerving Obedience

I have chosen the way of truth; I have set my heart on your laws.
I hold fast to your statutes, O LORD; do not let me be put to shame.
PSALM 119:30-31

Daniel was a leader. His leadership exhibited itself in many ways—
spiritually, politically and militarily. As an exile in a foreign land, he
had distinguished himself in extraordinary ways and risen to the
highest places of leadership. As a politician, he was not unaware of the
dangerous political maneuverings and jealousies that are part and par-
cel in an alien land.

Yet somehow, he managed to maintain his clear identity as a
God-fearing Jew, and still rise to the highest heights of one of the
most powerful kingdoms in the ancient world.

Jealous and ambitious, his political enemies began plotting his
downfall. Try as they could to find a flaw in his character, Daniel
stood secure. Finally, they devised a plan that centered on attacking
the core of his being: his faith.

Let's recall Daniel's faith . . .

Now Daniel so distinguished himself among the administrators and the satraps by his exceptional qualities that the king planned to set him over the whole kingdom. At this, the administrators and the satraps tried to find grounds for charges against Daniel in his conduct of government affairs, but they were unable to do so. They could find no corruption in him, because he was trustworthy and neither corrupt nor negligent. Finally these men said, "We will never find any basis for charges against this man Daniel unless it has something to do with the law of his God."

So the administrators and the satraps went as a group to the king and said: "O King Darius, live forever! The royal administrators, prefects, satraps, advisers and governors have all agreed that the king should issue an edict and enforce the decree that anyone who prays to any god or man during the next thirty days, except to you, O king, shall be thrown into the lions' den. Now, O king, issue the decree and put it in writing so that it cannot be altered—in accordance with the laws of the Medes and Persians, which cannot be repealed."

So King Darius put the decree in writing. Now when Daniel learned that the decree had been published, he went home to his upstairs room where the windows opened toward Jerusalem. Three times a day he got down on his knees and prayed, giving thanks to his God, just as he had done before (Daniel 6:3-10).

Now if I had been Daniel, I would have been very tempted to respond differently. I would have thought to myself, "Well, this plan was devised by the enemy to remove me from the position God has given me. Surely the Lord would not want that! I will simply pray in secret during these thirty days, and in this way the Lord and I will outsmart the enemy."

Or I might have thought, "God has commanded me to honor

the rulers who are over me, and so I will honor this command, and in doing so, I will honor the Lord."

Sounds reasonable, right?

It is dangerously easy to rationalize away the voice of the Holy Spirit—particularly when an overwhelming flood of other loud voices inundate us.

Whose Voice Will You Obey?

Voices arise from all directions when God asks us to act outside of conventional wisdom. Of course, the world offers education and experience to counter the unseen presence of God. "We have seen that this is what works," cries the world. "We have learned that what you are considering doesn't work," shout the textbooks of the worldly wise.

Political voices counsel us to take a vote and get a majority decision. Renaissance voices assure us that "the voice of the people is the voice of God." So we get boards to vote and ask committees to reach a consensus on whether or not to obey God's voice.

THIS NEW REVELATION REPLACES FOR THIS DAY AND TIME WHAT GODLY COUNSEL HAS BEEN THROUGH THE AGES. HUNGERING FOR WHAT'S NEW, IT'S DIFFICULT TO STAND ON ANCIENT TRUTHS THAT ARE IMMUTABLE.

Even spiritual voices proffer a wisdom that sounds mysterious and hauntingly enticing. We are standing firm in obedience to what God has said when, suddenly, someone appears with a new word and a savvy approach. This new revelation replaces for this day and time what godly counsel has been through the ages. Hungering for what's new, it's difficult to stand on ancient truths that are immutable.

The natural mind is overrun by what appears to be a computer virus multiplying itself infinitely with a myriad of reasons as to why we should waiver and change course. Rationalizations, like computer viruses, ultimately so confuse and confound our spiritual operating system that we cannot even "boot up" the word of God to discern right from wrong.

Daniel's mind must have been spinning with tempting reasons of why to obey the king and not God. I don't think Daniel reached his decision to continue praying in public view easily. I think he probably had to deeply consider what was required of him in this situation, and how he was to respond. He must have sorted through all of the natural, political, conventional and spiritual options available to him. But as in any maze, there is only one way out, no matter how many paths seem possible at first glance.

Tenacious Resolve

In the end, he knew what he had to do; he had to obey God rather than men. Here we have an early demonstration of the power of civil disobedience—perhaps better said as choosing heavenly obedience! Scripture reminds us:

> *You will keep him in perfect peace,*
> *Whose mind is stayed on You,*
> *Because he trusts in You* (Isa. 26:3 NKJV).

> *My brethren, count it all joy when you fall into various trials, knowing that the testing of your faith produces patience. But let patience have its perfect work, that you may be perfect and complete, lacking nothing. If any of you lacks wisdom, let him ask of God, who gives to all liberally and without reproach, and it will be given to him. But let him ask in faith, with no doubting, for*

he who doubts is like a wave of the sea driven and tossed by the wind. For let not that man suppose that he will receive anything from the Lord; he is a double-minded man, unstable in all his ways (James 1:2-8 NKJV).

Therefore take up the whole armor of God, that you may be able to withstand in the evil day, and having done all, to stand (Eph. 6:13 NKJV).

What is God calling you to obey Him in?

Are you willing to obey the Lord to your own hurt?

Are you willing to take the unpopular stand?

Are you offering the sacrifice of full obedience?

As I said earlier, it is interesting to note the "altars," the relationships, in these stories. Daniel was respected and trusted by the king. Even though the king was "not saved" (a pagan who worshipped idols), Daniel had developed a deep connection with him and had gained his respect and concern.

Eventually, the Lord took this relationship and used it to glorify Himself by miraculously saving Daniel and thereby revealing Himself to the king. The king then issued a decree declaring the reverence of God throughout all the land.

> "ARE WE VIEWING PEOPLE ONLY AS SOULS TO WIN, OR DO WE SEE THEM AS PEOPLE IN A PROCESS WITH GOD?"

Perhaps, if we were cultivating real relationships with unbelievers that had depth and integrity to them, there would also be opportunities in place for God to move more powerfully in those circumstances.

I fully believe in soul winning, but my question is, "Are we viewing people only as souls to win, or do we see them as people in a process with God?" And most importantly, "Are we willing to cultivate real relationship with them while they are on that journey?"

Will you sacrifice ambivalence and doubts for faith and stead-fastness?

Are you willing to sacrifice popular acclaim and political clout for steady obedience?

Will you ultimately obey God instead of trying to please others?

Carefully consider this plea from Paul: *"Therefore, my beloved brethren, be steadfast, immovable, always abounding in the work of the Lord, knowing that your labor is not in vain in the Lord"* (1Cor. 15:58 NKJV).

So, Daniel calls us to unswerving obedience, and right relationship with others along the way.

CHAPTER 10

BELIEVING THE
DREAM

*The Sacrifices of Waiting, Forgiveness and
Persistent Intercession*

*All my longings lie open before you, O Lord;
my sighing is not hidden from you.
I wait for you, O LORD; you will answer, O Lord my God.*

PSALM 38:9,15

It is so easy to hear Bible stories on Sunday mornings in a sermon or
a Sunday school class. It's a very different thing to grasp the vastness
and depth of the trauma, passion and emotion in these accounts.

Joseph's life brings me to tears every time I consider it deeply. We
think of him and his coat, and we fast forward to the happy ending.
But for years and years, Joseph had to live with the tension of his
prophetic dreams, and the way they had seemed to go terribly unful-
filled. Sold into slavery, wrongfully accused, cast into prison and forgotten by the king's servant whom he had helped, Joseph certainly
had cause to forget the dream, believing it all to be foolishness, and
to live in bitterness and distrust.

Again, it's easy to consider the story briefly and abstractly. But take a moment to apply the story to YOU.

What dreams are you still waiting on?

What hopes are you still cherishing even though they seem a million miles away from reality?

Or have you given up already?

Have you despaired of believing in the word, or dream, because it didn't come about when or how you thought it would?

And who has hurt you? Who has betrayed you? Who has sold your friendship into slavery—hurting you out of jealousy or spite? How is your heart toward them?

If we are to bring an acceptable sacrifice to God, one of the most poignant offerings we can bring are the dreams we feel He has spoken to us. Those dreams, time and time again, need to be laid on the altar and filled with fresh hope. Sometimes a dream requires more than faith to lay it down; it requires hope to pick it back up again after we have died to it at the altar.

Offering up our dreams daily before the Lord—recognizing that really those dreams are His and that they came from Him—brings a constant stream from heaven that *purifies* our intentions and *clarifies* our pursuits. If we get fixated on something happening in just the time and way we planned, we will miss the fact that God fulfills His word to us in the midst of our spiritual journey.

However, if we lose sight of the dream and cast it aside, we will often neglect or forget to pick it up again.

The Sacrifice of Forgiveness

For if you forgive men their trespasses, your heavenly Father will also forgive you. But if you do not forgive men their trespasses, neither will your Father forgive your trespasses (Matt. 6:14-15 NKJV).

Joseph's life speaks to us of a tenacious faith that continually embraced hope in God despite all that came to discourage him. Rather than becoming bitter, Joseph brought to his altar of worship a sacrifice of comprehensive forgiveness, recognizing that even those who had hurt him didn't fully realize what they had done.

Of course, if we grow from those hurts, if we learn from those experiences and become better for them, then they have significantly helped us achieve the goals of our heart. Joseph repaired the altar of relationship between him and his brothers, rather than allowing it to stay in ruins.

Which one of us cannot look back on painful experiences we have gone through and realize that those times have really formed us and fashioned us and made us better?

I think of a quote from my good friend, Dr. Joseph Umidi, a theologian and true leader in the body of Christ. Joe says, "On the other side of conflict, courageously faced, lies the blessing of God."

If we can remember in the midst of our struggles to hold on to the God of the dream, the dream of God, and to walk in loving forgiveness of those who have hurt us along the way, we are walking in a great pathway toward godly success.

The Sacrifice of Persistent Intercession

I rise before dawn and cry for help;
I have put my hope in your word.
My eyes stay open through the watches of the night,
that I may meditate on your promises
(Psalm 119:147-148).

All of us believe, theoretically, in the power of prayer. But many times we fail to see that the Scriptures teach us that sometimes, prayer is answered only after long seasons of persistent intercession.

Hannah was a woman whose husband loved her very much, but who had great pain in her heart because she could not conceive a child. Year after year, she would go up to the house of the Lord to seek Him, and year after year she was taunted by her husband's second wife.

How many times did she cry herself to sleep?

How many times did she want to quit believing that God loved her or cared for her?

How many times did she wonder if she had done something wrong, something terrible to offend God?

How many times did she hope and wonder if perhaps she was pregnant, and then, every month, have her hopes dashed again?

HANNAH'S DESPERATION DROVE HER TO THE LORD. SHE ALLOWED HER PAIN TO BRING HER TO THE PLACE OF PRAYER. ONCE IN THE PLACE OF PRAYER, SHE WENT DEEPER, AND ENTERED INTO A COVENANT WITH THE LORD.

Remember, Scripture is *real* stories about *real* people facing *real* situations— many times with *real* pain. And if our belief in God is to become more than just nice sounding phrases, we have to press in to the reality of the stories to draw strength from the testimony that they have left for us.

And the difficult thing about Hannah's story, the thing that does not sit well with us, is that the Word says that the Lord had closed her womb.

Why? Why would God do this?

Isn't He good? Doesn't He want to heal and help?

Why would He let Hannah endure this suffering?

The Scripture is silent. It provides no answers to these questions.

It is interesting to note, however, that Hannah's desperation drove her to the Lord. She allowed her pain to bring her to the place of prayer. Once in the place of prayer, she went deeper, and entered into a covenant with the Lord.

She said, *"Lord, if you will give me a son—the most precious thing that I am longing for—I will offer him to you as a sacrifice. I will give him back to You, to serve in Your house all the days of his life"* (cf.1 Sam. 1:11).

Desperation produced prayer.

Prayer produced relationship.

Relationship produced a sacrifice and a covenant.

God had a Plan

I believe that God got what He was after. Isn't it possible that in this time of great backsliding by Hophni and Phineas (in a time when God could not allow Eli's line to continue to serve anymore in the temple) that the Lord was looking for one to walk before Him in righteousness? And, before he was formed in his mother's womb, He saw Samuel, loved him, and decided to set him apart for His own pleasure.

But to have a chosen vessel set apart for the Lord is not an easy thing. The world is full of distractions and opportunities that vie for our attention and the energy of our life. How could the Lord mark Samuel's life with destiny so that he would be unmistakably set apart for Him?

Could it be that the desperation preceding his birth was the Lord's pause; which allowed Hannah time to realize that this son was not born to work in the fields or to be a merchant or a shepherd?

Perhaps you feel uncomfortable with the notion that God would wait for anything. But God waited for the "fullness of time" to be realized before Christ was born. Even before Christ, God waited patiently for Noah to build the ark (1 Peter 3:20 NLT).

Could it be that this delay, what Bob Sorge calls "the fire of delayed answers," was allowed so that from his conception, Samuel would be set apart for the Lord?

Now, Samuel would realize from the time of his earliest memories that his life was different; it was marked with purpose and destiny.

And what about Hannah, you say? She had brought her sacrifice of persistent prayer to God along with her tears and pain. She had kept the flame ablaze before God.

So, after this delay, how did Hannah really feel about God?

Is God so cruel and unfeeling as to exploit her pain, just so He could have His way?

Is God so unfeeling that He uses, deliberately, the pain of barrenness to work His purpose?

I think we should let Hannah speak for herself . . .

Then Hannah prayed and said:
"My heart rejoices in the LORD;
in the LORD my horn is lifted high.
My mouth boasts over my enemies,
for I delight in your deliverance.

There is no one holy like the LORD;
there is no one besides you;
there is no Rock like our God.

Do not keep talking so proudly
or let your mouth speak such arrogance,
for the LORD is a God who knows,
and by him deeds are weighed.

The bows of the warriors are broken,
but those who stumbled are armed with strength.

Those who were full hire themselves out for food,
but those who were hungry hunger no more.
She who was barren has borne seven children,
but she who has had many sons pines away.

The LORD brings death and makes alive;
he brings down to the grave and raises up.
The LORD sends poverty and wealth;
he humbles and he exalts.

He raises the poor from the dust
and lifts the needy from the ash heap;
he seats them with princes
and has them inherit a throne of honor.

For the foundations of the earth are the LORD's;
upon them he has set the world.
He will guard the feet of his saints,
but the wicked will be silenced in darkness.

It is not by strength that one prevails;
those who oppose the LORD will be shattered.
He will thunder against them from heaven;
the LORD will judge the ends of the earth.

He will give strength to his king
and exalt the horn of his anointed"
(1 Sam. 2:1-10).

Does that sound like an unsatisfied heart? Of course not. Hannah broke through to victory . . . *and what a victory it was!* Her son was not just any son; her son was being trained in the house of God under Eli the priest!

Do you feel the pride in that Jewish mother's heart? And in the years to come, she would know that her son was the one who took Eli's place, and eventually the one who anointed King David. Do you think she even REMEMBERED her pain? No—she had the garment of praise instead of the spirit of heaviness!

> DO YOU THINK SHE EVEN REMEMBERED HER PAIN? NO— SHE HAD THE GARMENT OF PRAISE INSTEAD OF THE SPIRIT OF HEAVINESS!

Then the Lord multiplied her and she had five more children as well.

God's Plan for You

Beloved, if we respond to our barren places in the right way . . . .

If we pray out of the place of our barrenness to the God who is there, and trust Him, and trust His ways...

If we make covenant with Him in place of the reality of our pain . . . .

He will come to us.

He will answer us.

He will hear us.

He will incline unto us
and bring us through into life and victory.

Don't let delayed dreams or answers to your prayers quench the flame you are keeping at God's altar.

Keep the flame burning bright.

Delay simply deepens your desperation and increases your desire to keep the flame ablaze.

CHAPTER 11

REDEEMING THE TIME

The Sacrifice of Our Hands

May the favor of the Lord our God rest upon us;
establish the work of our hands for us—
yes, establish the work of our hands.

PSALM 90:17

I love Scripture for many reasons. One of which is this: *it's so real and practical.* Those who find the Bible irrelevant simply have not taken the time to see how pointedly and exactly it speaks to all situations of life.

Our desire is to bring an acceptable sacrifice. We are seeking right order in our lives so that our intercession may be effective in this generation to prepare the way for the Lord. We must bring into pure scrutiny our hearts, our motives, our emotions and our prayer lives. It's essential for us to daily examine the sincerity of our motives.

Who do you work for?

As I travel the world, I meet countless people who come to me and say, "Robert, please pray for me. I am really feeling called to full-time min-

istry." Not a week goes by that this does not happen. Somehow, we have
created this concept of "full-time ministry"; that it is a special, elite, nir-
vana-like place where we float around on a
cloud of anointing and special feelings.

I FEEL LIKE ASKING
THESE PEOPLE, "HAVE
YOU TRIED BEING A
FULL-TIME
CHRISTIAN YET?"

I feel like asking these people, "Have
you tried being a full-time Christian yet?"
Being a Christian *is* a full-time ministry.
What some people really mean when they
refer to full-time ministry is that they
want to work for a ministry or a church .
. . *and they want to be paid what a vocation in the world pays.*

Consider this. Vocation means *calling*. We are *called* to serve
Christ wherever we *work*. Paul earned a living by tent making. He
worked full-time, all the time, in living for Christ. He didn't need a
salary from a ministry organization to validate his service. Paul wrote
in Philippians 1:21, *"For me, to live is Christ . . ."* That sounds full-
time. Money, salary, compensation, benefits and the like were not
part of his consideration. His calling was to Christ in the office of an
apostle. Earning money was simply part of his vocation.

Ministry is spelled W-O-R-K. Especially end time, apostolic
ministry. If we are really living in the last days (and I believe that we
are) then we need to realize that we are preparing for momentous
times ahead. We need to be like the "sons of Issachar" who understood the times and knew what Israel should do (1 Chr. 12:32).

Read some of the description of the "full-time ministry" by Paul.

*I have worked much harder, been in prison more frequently, been
flogged more severely, and been exposed to death again and again.
Five times I received from the Jews the forty lashes minus one.
Three times I was beaten with rods, once I was stoned, three times
I was shipwrecked, I spent a night and a day in the open sea, I*

have been constantly on the move. I have been in danger from rivers, in danger from bandits, in danger from my own countrymen, in danger from Gentiles; in danger in the city, in danger in the country, in danger at sea; and in danger from false brothers. I have labored and toiled and have often gone without sleep; I have known hunger and thirst and have often gone without food; I have been cold and naked. Besides everything else, I face daily the pressure of my concern for all the churches (2 Cor. 11:23b-28).

Friends, building Kingdom lifestyles and living out Kingdom values is not easy. It is not for the faint of heart. Really living out the message of Jesus takes work, effort, pain, selflessness, endurance and —you guessed it—more work!

Do we want to offer an acceptable sacrifice? Do we want to really see *change* in this generation? Are we desperate for God to move and ready to pay any price to see holy revolution grip our time as it has in days of old?

Then let's be prepared to make the sacrifice of our hands.

TO LIVE IN THE KINGDOM IS NOT TO "FIT IN" TIME FOR THE LORD. INSTEAD, IT IS TO RECOGNIZE THAT HE IS THE LORD OF ALL TIME AND THAT WE ARE RESPONSIBLE FOR HOW WE STEWARD WHAT HE GIVES US.

Time as a Gift

Time is the most precious thing there is. None of us feel we have enough of it. All of us wish for more of it. The technological world works furiously to try to provide more gadgets for us to simplify our lives and increase our time, yet we feel as though we have less and less of it.

But Jesus does not come and ask us to fit Him into our world. Rather, He wants to *become our world*. To live in the Kingdom is not to "fit in" time for the Lord. Instead, it is to recognize that He is the Lord of all time and that we are responsible for how we steward what He gives us.

Jesus' life is the perfect example of wholly living one's life in God's Kingdom. See a typical example of how he lived his life.

> *As he went along, he saw a man blind from birth. His disciples asked him, "Rabbi, who sinned, this man or his parents, that he was born blind?"*
>
> *"Neither this man nor his parents sinned," said Jesus, "but this happened so that the work of God might be displayed in his life. As long as it is day, we must do the work of him who sent me. Night is coming, when no one can work. While I am in the world, I am the light of the world."*
>
> *Having said this, he spit on the ground, made some mud with the saliva, and put it on the man's eyes. "Go," he told him, "wash in the Pool of Siloam" (this word means Sent). So the man went and washed, and came home seeing* (John 9:1-7).

"As he went along," the scripture says, he encountered the blind man, and his disciples asked about him. What was Jesus doing here? Was he healing? Yes. Was he discipling his followers? Yes. Was he evangelizing? Yes. A few verses later, he confronts religious society.

> *Jesus heard that they had thrown him out, and when he found him, he said, "Do you believe in the Son of Man?"*
>
> *"Who is he, sir?" the man asked. "Tell me so that I may believe in him."*
>
> *Jesus said, "You have now seen him; in fact, he is the one speaking with you."*
>
> *Then the man said, "Lord, I believe," and he worshiped him.*
>
> *Jesus said, "For judgment I have come into this world, so that*

the blind will see and those who see will become blind."

Some Pharisees who were with him heard him say this and asked, "What? Are we blind too?"

Jesus said, "If you were blind, you would not be guilty of sin; but now that you claim you can see, your guilt remains (John 9:35-41).

In other words, Jesus lived his life intentionally. He did not have a "to do" list, which spelled out what times he was going to teach, which times he was going to evangelize and which times he was going to confront society. Rather, He released the Kingdom of God reality that was in Him and projected it out into every circumstance He encountered. The Kingdom of God was literally coming OUT of Him, like salt and light—seasoning and illuminating everything and everyone He touched.

Rather than setting aside times to do "holy things," I believe God wants us to redeem every opportunity by sanctifying it with His presence and power. His Kingdom is expanded when we consecrate every step we take as holy unto Him.

Using Time Wisely

Many things in and of themselves are not intrinsically holy or profane, but it is how we approach them and what we do with them that makes the difference.

Do you want to go out with some friends for some coffee or dessert? Fine! But how will your conversation be during that time?

What will the purpose of the time be?

Will it be only superficial?

Will there be anything of the Kingdom of God in your time?

Will Jesus and His purpose be at the center of your time?

I am not saying that every experience has to be "super-spiritual," but I am saying that, for *keepers of the flame,* for citizens of God's Kingdom, every experience should be a holy one. We need to under-

THE KINGDOM OF
GOD WAS LITERALLY
COMING OUT OF
HIM, LIKE SALT AND
LIGHT—SEASONING
AND ILLUMINATING
EVERYTHING AND
EVERYONE HE
TOUCHED.

stand life as an experience set apart with higher purpose. The presence of God and an understanding of His purpose should sanctify all we do. When this happens, our time begins to multiply.

Once, when my wife and I had rented a movie, we decided to have five or six young friends over whom we were discipling. The movie was very emotional. It told the story of a boy in conflict with his father and the struggles that he had. It was a very moving film. However, in typical Hollywood fashion, I began to recognize a very anti-family, anti-father subplot in the movie. While it was not at all obvious on the surface, because of the poignant story line, the fact was that the movie communicated a world-view that was very anti-God.

When the movie ended, everyone was making comments on how good a movie it was and how all had enjoyed it. I began asking a few probing questions, pointing out some of what I thought I had observed. Several other comments were made, and then the conversation moved into the deep subject of fatherhood and its relation to the establishment of value systems and morality. We had powerful, meaningful conversation because we sought to wisely steward the valuable gift of time.

The night might have been nothing more than an evening of relaxation, which would have subtly left the negative message of the movie unconfronted. Instead, it became a night in which we deepened our relationships, shared honestly and saw the Kingdom of God increase because we used our time intentionally.

Again, who demonstrated this more than Jesus? It was often at parties and dinners that he did His miracles and released His teachings. His spirituality and Kingdom message were released through Him wherever He was. Likewise, our spirituality should not be just a Sunday morning experience.

EVERY DECISION REGARDING OUR TIME IS AN ETERNAL ONE. WE ARE INVESTING INTO EITHER THE KINGDOM OR THE WORLD THE MOST PRECIOUS SEED THAT WE HAVE—OUR TIME.

Who is Lord of Your Time?

Jesus is Lord of our time all of the time. When we are on the job for which we are paid, He is Lord. When we are with our families and friends, He is Lord. When we are resting and being refreshed, He is Lord. When we are in the midst of spiritual disciplines, ministering spiritual gifts, worshipping or playing, He is Lord.

Wasting time is simply using this precious gift in a way that doesn't honor, glorify or serve Him. At times, people waste time at church or in a worship service. They are *using* time for something religious but not *redeeming* the time for His purposes and glory. In other words, are you doing with your time what the Lord has directed at each and every moment, or are you using time selfishly and foolishly?

People who are stressed out in ministry are often using their time foolishly or for their own glory. People who find themselves burdened and depressed by ministry are doing the wrong things for the wrong reasons.

Time is the currency of life. You spend it on what's important to you. I know pastors and evangelists, music ministers and worship leaders who have lost spouses and children because they wasted time working when they should have been investing time in their families. Likewise, I have seen some in ministry waste time being lazy at home while the needs of God's people were neglected or ignored, the lost were not being evangelized and the poor were not served.

There has never been more opportunity to waste time than today. We waste time with television by giving our attention to ungodly standards and unwise voices. Even the commercials on TV communicate value systems that are totally contrary to God's Kingdom.

It is so frustrating to see so many believers jealously and selfishly guarding their time, but not really giving it to the Lord and His purposes. The excuse is given, "I need some time to myself" or, "I need some down time," but what is really being said is that time is needed for television, for going to the mall or for other pursuits that are not advancing the Kingdom of God.

As long as we are trying to "fit God in" to our modern, American lifestyles, we will not enter into the Kingdom work of redeeming our time and submitting it to the King and His Kingdom. *Every decision regarding our time is an eternal one.* We are investing into either the Kingdom or the world the most precious seed that we have—our time.

A Time to Choose

If the Lordship of Jesus is to come to the deepest places of our lives, then we will need to yield to the Lord the rights to our time. This will mean making choices to avoid time-wasters, which (though not inherently evil) are not the best use of our resources.

They are good ideas but not God ideas.

They have momentary impact but lack lasting significance.

It's time to decide to only do those things that last for eternity. And what are the criteria for such "holy" uses of time? Jesus sets the standard for the use of time:

Then Jesus answered and said to them, "Most assuredly, I say to you, the Son can do nothing of Himself, but what He sees the Father do; for whatever He does, the Son also does in like manner" (John 5:19 NKJV).

So, we only do what God shows us to do; we only say what the Father tells us to say. The Eternal God reveals to us how to use our time in such a way that we store up treasures in heaven instead of doing those things that will eventually fade away.

At this hour of human history, we as believers CANNOT afford to waste time on neutral activities. We must be redeeming every moment and yielding it to Christ and His purposes.

Who is Lord of Your Possessions?

Another sacrifice relating to the work of our hands, which we must bring to the Lord is the wrongful sense of ownership we have over our possessions. We must surrender our covetous desire to grasp that which is not ours. I mentioned earlier A.W. Tozer's vow of "own nothing." We are simply stewards of things the Lord has given us, and we should hold lightly to the earthly things we have, being willing at any moment to use them for the Lord.

Often, Eagles' Wings is involved in coordinating regional conferences designed to equip the Church. We seek housing for the staff of our ministry team so that we can be better stewards of God's money and not have to spend a lot on hotels.

It amazes me, over and over, how difficult it is to find believers in churches who will open their homes to these ministers. Even in very large congregations (in fact, sometimes especially in large congregations) it seems impossible to find even a few who follow the biblical injunction to practice hospitality. Paul writes, *"Share with God's peo-*

ple who are in need. Practice hospitality" (Rom. 12:13). Other biblical injunctions are:

> *Offer hospitality to one another without grumbling. Each one should use whatever gift he has received to serve others, faithfully administering God's grace in its various forms* (1 Peter 4:9-10). *We ought therefore to show hospitality to such men so that we may work together for the truth* (3 John 1:8).

> *Do not forget to entertain strangers, for by so doing some people have entertained angels without knowing it* (Heb. 13:2).

The principle of hospitality should extend beyond our homes to all our resources. Are we open with all of the things entrusted to us, freely sharing with the community of faith and with those in need?

Putting our time and possessions on the altar enables us to keep the flame ablaze in doing that which glorifies God and ministers to the deep needs of others in His name and power.

CHAPTER 12

SOWING AND REAPING

The Sacrifice of Diligence

*Let us not become weary in doing good, for at the proper time
we will reap a harvest if we do not give up.*

GALATIANS 6:9

Americans often operate under the mindset to consume instead of give; to expect comfort instead of sacrifice. Instead of being selfless, we find ourselves in selfish, self-centered work that satisfies our desires for the moment instead of pleasing God for eternity. The overriding question posed before most work is, "What's in it for me?"

The Kingdom of God mandates a servant mentality. The overriding question is, "How can I serve?"

The orientation of too many in the American Church is that the church exists to serve them and meet their needs. Within that group, we may have a core of volunteers who help get things done, but usually that group is a very small percentage of the whole congregation, and even they are only able to function because the paid staff members are in place giving oversight and direction.

The Kingdom of God is about an army of servant leaders, each esteeming one another above themselves, and ready for the *real* work of taking the Gospel of Jesus into the highways and the byways. Believers must treat their areas of responsibility not as a hobby that they can get to when it's convenient, but rather as a divine assignment in God's kingdom plan.

BELIEVERS SHOULD BE SETTING THE STANDARD AND WORKING WITH ALL DILIGENCE AND MIGHT—EVEN MORE SO AS WE SEE THE DAY OF THE LORD APPROACHING!

Diligence. Excellence. Productivity. These values, which were so much a part of the founding of America because they were rooted in a Puritan understanding of God's Word, need to be recaptured by us today. We should not settle for the lowest common denominator in the criteria for accomplishing our work. We should not be reflections of our culture. We should be a radiant light shining into the darkness of our surroundings.

Pride of craftsmanship and the joy of hard work are disappearing from America and the Western nations of the world. We have become lazy and irresponsible, forgetting what it really means to work. This should not be the case in the House of God! Believers should be setting the standard and working with all diligence and might—even more so as we see the day of the Lord approaching! We must put up a spiritual fight in our generation to instill in the people of God a mentality that knows how to work and realizes that hard work, without complaining, is glorifying to God.

Work Completed with Biblical Excellence

Hard work is sacrifice. We place our work on the altar so that an exemplary light shines from that work to others in the Church and the world. Whatever we do, we should be able to say with Paul,

"Imitate me, just as I also imitate Christ" (1 Cor. 11:1 NKJV). What does such consecration and commitment to doing His work with excellence look like?

Taking initiative with obedience. John Maxwell says, "You can't go up until you get up." That may sound too simplistic, but the truth is that too many Christians often talk the talk but never get around to the walk. They talk about the importance of praying, studying the Word, giving, worshipping, witnessing, working and serving; but they fail to start most of the projects God sets before them. Often, they procrastinate starting and, in so doing, lose the momentum of the *kairos* moment for that particular work.

What else hinders starting?

1. *Unwillingness.* At times, it takes us so long to decide to obey that we actually lapse into disobedience and even rebellion. Instead of praying, "Lord, I am willing," we pray, "Lord make me willing to be willing." When the sacrifice of work is diligently made by *keepers of the flame,* we have already committed to the task even before the Lord has revealed the specifics. Too often we want to know all that the work involves before we take the first step. We pray, "God, show me all that this assignment involves," instead of praying, "God, here I am. Send me now" (see Isaiah 6).

2. *Timidity.* God has given us a spirit of love, power and a sound mind; not a spirit of timidity (2 Tim. 1:7). The early Christians were marked by love and by a power that included boldness to take risks. Every faith initiative involves risk. Work may demand that we make a sacrificial investment of time, effort and money before we ever see any return. Yet, with sacrificial investment comes the risk of losing something. Paradoxically, Jesus reminds us that it's only in losing life that we gain it.

3. *Personal agendas.* When we begin to work, submitting to authority, we must lay aside personal agendas. That can be difficult. We

may enter our work with expectations that may be unrealistic or self-ish. Kingdom work is not about want we want; it is passion for what He wants.

Remember this:

- *Keepers of the flame work out of conviction, not preference.*
  Because of personal agendas, a worker may prefer not to show up on time, not to do the assigned task in the assigned way or not to work for another's success. But *keepers of the flame* work to show themselves steadfast, loyal, dependable and selfless. Rights are transformed into privileges and privileges come as grace, not rewards.

- *Keepers of the flame have matured as workers to the point that they are submitting to another's authority and working for another's success.* The servant leader ultimately rejoices in the success of others instead of striving for personal glory and success. Paradoxically, when we help others succeed in the Kingdom; we discover personal success and prosperity.

Being motivated to please God, not man. In their work, *keepers of the flame:*

- Look to godly leaders for *Direction* and look to God for *Affirmation* (Prov. 3:6).

- Look to godly leaders for *Casting vision* and to God for *Provision* (Phil. 4:19).

- Look to godly leaders for *Motivation* and to God for *Inspiration* (2 Tim. 3:16-17).

- Look to godly leaders for *Participation* and to God for *Foundation* (1 Cor. 3:9-15).

Paul reminds us that we work to please God, not man (1 Thess. 2:4ff). Our motives are never to accept glory but rather to glorify God in all our work.

Be a Laboring Levite. *"Instead, appoint the Levites to be in charge* *of the tabernacle of the Testimony—over all its furnishings and everything belonging to it. They are to carry the tabernacle and all its furnishings; they are to take care of it and encamp around it"* (Num. 1: 50).

The Levites of the Old Testament were real laborers; not just in prayer, but also in deed. They were given practical responsibilities to set up and tear down the tabernacle as it moved from place to place. As a Covenant Priesthood, let us take all of our labors, whether prayerful or practical, seriously.

Exerting effort with excellence. Scripture warns against laziness (Prov. 19:15, Eccl. 10:18). It's time to decide that perspiration must follow inspiration. We work hard and we rest in order to be revived and refreshed. The effort we exert demonstrates that we will settle for nothing less than our best.

Valuing teamwork. Paul makes a fitting analogy of the Church being like the body in 1 Cor. 12. Our work must team with others by building on their strengths instead of criticizing their weaknesses. When we encourage others, we will receive back from them what we have given. Paul reminds us in Galatians 6 that sowing to the Spirit brings a like harvest. Those who work hard at building a team discover that having friends keeps them from failing.

> *Two people can accomplish more than twice as much as one; they get a better return for their labor. If one person falls, the other can reach out and help. But people who are alone when they fall are in real trouble. And on a cold night, two under the same blanket can gain warmth from each other. But how can one be warm alone? A person standing alone can be attacked and defeated, but two can stand back-to-back and conquer. Three are even better, for a triple-braided cord is not easily broken* (Eccl. 4:9-12 NLT).

Raising the bar. Go above and beyond whatever's been done before. Refuse to let early failure stifle your effort. Keep taking the test until you pass instead of settling for the lie, "It's better to have tried and failed than never tried at all." Overcome until victory becomes the norm and not the surprise. Stop complaining about how hard your work is or how much is expected of you. *Keepers of the flame* are overcomers (Rev. 2-3).

Expecting productivity. We work to see results. Just as a farmer sows seed with the expectation of a future harvest, so our work involves both sowing and reaping, to the end that we see a Kingdom harvest of souls, healing, deliverance and people equipped and raised up in leadership (Luke 9-10).

Being Realistic. Remember that growth and results take time to produce. Work that is rushed through often produces more frustration and more work. Excellence involves efficiency but not wasteful haste. Give yourself enough time to produce the most abundant results.

Staying focused. Set goals on a reasonable timeline and stick to it. Fix your eyes on Jesus so that you will push through every hindrance. Don't quit, give up or make excuses. Be disciplined. Set a pace fast enough so that when obstacles slow you, you will not stop (Heb. 12).

Receiving constructive input and counsel. (Prov. 24:6). Learn from the mistakes and experience of others. Ask for help and for what you need. Never resent input even from your enemies. They see your weaknesses much more clearly than you do.

Making appropriate corrections. Change when change is needed. Be flexible standing firm on truth and godly principles. Replace pride with humility so that what you do doesn't define who you are (Prov. 15:5, 10).

Persevering without encouragement. If those in authority over you can't affirm you, encourage yourself in the Lord. Give glory to God each step of the way. Be satisfied in the fruit of your labor, not in the praise of others (Rom. 12:9-21).

Finishing the job. Finishing produces results. Keep trying until you get it right and get it done. Don't let up at the end. The hardest work comes during the final harvest (1 Cor. 9:24-27).

The sacrifice of work is encouraged by Paul in this way, *"So, my dear brothers and sisters, be strong and steady, always enthusiastic about the Lord's work, for you know that nothing you do for the Lord is ever useless"* (1 Cor. 15:58 NLT).

Keepers of the flame must work to keep the flame burning. The work isn't to earn our salvation or calling. Christ has already provided that place through His sacrifice. Rather, we do the work in order to hear this: *"Well done, good and faithful servant; you have been faithful over a few things, I will make you ruler over many things. Enter into the joy of your lord"* (Mt. 25:23 NKJV).

CHAPTER 13

WITH OUR FACE TOWARD THE SUNRISE

The Sacrifice of Unrealized Promises

The LORD will fulfill his purpose for me;
your love, O LORD, endures forever—
do not abandon the works of your hands.

PSALM 138:8

There is one final sacrifice I want to touch on before we move on to other aspects of keeping the flame. The eleventh chapter of Hebrews is the famous passage that deals with the power of faith.

This chapter details the glorious accounts of saints who persevered and overcame by faith. Name by name, the heroes of faith are recounted, along with the details of their victories. The author summarizes all of these accounts this way:

> *All these people were still living by faith when they died. They did*
> *not receive the things promised; they only saw them and wel-*
> *comed them from a distance. And they admitted that they were*
> *aliens and strangers on earth. People who say such things show*
> *that they are looking for a country of their own. If they had been*
> *thinking of the country they had left, they would have had oppor-*

tunity to return. Instead, they were longing for a better country—a heavenly one. Therefore God is not ashamed to be called their God, for he has prepared a city for them (Hebrews 11:13-16).

What does this mean? They were still living by faith when they died! They finished strong. Again, I have to encourage us to see Scripture not as we have idealized it, but rather in all of its raw beauty.

How many of these heroes of faith never really saw the full realization of the vision, promise or dream that God had deposited in their hearts?

> HOW MANY OF THESE HEROES OF FAITH NEVER REALLY SAW THE FULL REALIZATION OF THE VISION, PROMISE OR DREAM THAT GOD HAD DEPOSITED IN THEIR HEARTS?

How many only saw by faith the invisible but never experienced in time and space the visible manifestation of what God had promised?

As *keepers of the flame,* are we willing to build the altar and make the sacrifices without seeing in our lifetimes all that we have hoped and believed for?

Consider this:

- **Abraham** was promised a great nation that would spring forth from Isaac, but Abraham died only seeing a seed of that nation—his son Isaac!
- **Moses** faithfully led the people of God forth into salvation and victory, bringing them ever nearer to the Promised Land, but in the end could not enter it himself.
- **David** saw the Temple, the House of God, in his spirit and longed to build the resting place for the Lord whom He loved. But the Lord said no. God said that Solomon, not David, would actually build the Temple. David could only see it in his heart.

- **The prophets,** while in exile, spoke of the time that Israel would enter back into her own land, but died, many martyred, never seeing their words validated.
- **Simeon** waited his whole life to see the "consolation of Israel," and held the child in his arms. Yet he never heard Jesus preach a message or saw Him heal the sick or raise the dead. Simeon only saw the seed.
- **Jesus** Himself, how could He suffer as He did, and endure? The Bible says, *"Jesus, who for the joy set before Him, endured the cross, despising the shame"* (cf. Heb. 12). Jesus' eyes, the real eyes of His heart, were not set on temporal circumstances, but on an eternal reality. He saw the joy that was coming, the fulfillment of His Father's word, and so He had faith to endure the cross.

Beloved, the Bible is simple, but it is not simplistic. It is not a quick fix guide offering easy answers. But it does offer real answers.

How could these all endure what they endured and still *die in faith?*

The Reality of the Invisible

Therefore we do not lose heart. Even though our outward man is perishing, yet the inward man is being renewed day by day. For our light affliction, which is but for a moment, is working for us a far more exceeding and eternal weight of glory, while we do not look at the things which are seen, but at the things which are not seen. For the things which are seen are temporary, but the things which are not seen are eternal (2 Cor. 4:16-18 NKJV).

For the heroes of faith and the *keepers of the flame,* spiritual sight must become *reality* for us. I'm sure you have seen optical illusions. What you think you see isn't really what's there. You have to look with a different perspective and new understanding if you are to see what's really there. What's visible is illusion; what's invisible is real.

When the heroes of the faith had seen something in the spirit and when it had been tested and tried and confirmed by God and His Word, they knew that it was real. They saw it. They believed it. It didn't matter to them when or even *if* it manifested in the natural realm during their lifetimes.

God's Word invites us to offer up every unrealized promise as a "sacrifice of praise," not out of a weepy sense of loss that the promise was not fulfilled. Instead, He invites us to lift up our eyes to the hills, to the mountain of faith, and see with the eyes of our hearts the reality of His plan that works outside of human time. God invites us to walk by faith and to see that His word is fulfilled generation to generation.

Can We Take a Step of Faith?

Do we dare believe whatever God shows us as we sacrifice in praise?

Are we willing to join the ancient *"keepers of the flame"* by walk-

BELOVED, THE BIBLE IS SIMPLE, BUT IT IS NOT SIMPLISTIC. IT IS NOT A QUICK FIX GUIDE OFFERING EASY ANSWERS. BUT IT DOES OFFER REAL ANSWERS.

ing in faith? Consider this: After listing all the heroes of the faith, Hebrews 12:1 concludes, *"Therefore we also, since we are surrounded by so great a cloud of witnesses . . . ."* Imagine that. We are surrounded by the ancient heroes of faith as we walk by faith seeing the invisible. What does this mean?

I believe with all my heart that Abraham, today, is seeing his descendents, as numerous as the stars and as plentiful as the sand on the seashore. Abraham is in that cloud of witnesses surrounding us.

I believe that Moses, even now, is walking all over the Promised

Land, enjoying the fragrance of its milk and honey. Moses is in that cloud of witnesses surrounding us.

I believe David was present when the *shechinah* (cloud of glory) filled the Temple as his son, Solomon, dedicated it to the Lord. And I believe that even today, he is standing over the Temple Mount, looking for the Temple to be restored once again. David joins us in that cloud of witnesses.

I believe Simeon was there when Jesus walked on the water, and healed Jairus' daughter, and taught the Sermon on the Mount. Simeon is by your side and mine in that cloud of witnesses.

And we know that Jesus, our High Priest, at this very moment, is *"ever living to make intercession for us"* (Heb. 7:25). He is making ready the bridal chamber, and is filled with anticipation as the consummation of the ages draws near.

The Journey of Faith

Friend, you are not a physical being who has temporary spiritual experiences. You are a spiritual being who is having a temporary physical experience. See with the eyes of faith the purposes of God being worked through the intercession of your life. The purpose He was bringing forth went far beyond Abraham having many descendents, or David building a physical temple, or Simeon seeing the Messiah. He is working, through physical circumstances, a far deeper and more enduring expression of His Kingdom.

God is reconciling the world to Himself (2 Cor. 5:19) and bringing all things together in Messiah. He is making His enemies His footstool (1 Cor. 15) and bringing light and healing to the nations. God is birthing a new heaven and a new earth (Rev. 21).

Your trials and difficulties are not about you. They are about God's plan and purpose being brought forth through you. Wrestle against your doubts and walk in faith for that impossible dream, vision, purpose and plan that God has deposited in you.

Look for *that*.

Understand *that*.

Wait for *that*.

See *that*.

Join in with all creation, which is groaning and waiting for the revelation of God's glory (Rev. 8).

Don't understand your trials in terms of only the natural, human, temporal element of it. Our light afflictions are working out a weight

See with the eyes of faith the purposes of God being worked through the intercession of your life.

of glory as the invisible is being manifested into the visible through our prayers and obedient sacrifices.

Realize that GOD is at work in your situation, bringing about His purposes.

Remember the struggles, cries and groaning supplications of Hannah and what they produced. The prophet Samuel was birthed and through him, David's throne was established.

And who knows but that out of your barrenness and desperation, will come a covenant sacrifice, which will produce a prophet to anoint a king.

Keep the flame. Make the sacrifice. By faith, see the invisible. Look around you at the altar; the great cloud of witnesses cheering you on.

Remember the sacrifices they made and how, if they had it to do all over again, they would make a hundred more.

Remember—behind that cloud of witnesses on the horizon is the sun; and the promise that, after the long night of pain and tears, the day will surely dawn.

THE FIRE

I have come to bring fire on the earth,
and how I wish it were already kindled!

LUKE 12:49

From Moses meeting with God in the flame of the burning bush, to the seven eternal flames that blaze around the throne of God, fire has always been an elemental part of the story of God and man. Fire is something man cannot live without, and yet it also holds great danger for us. This is a perfect picture of God, who is our "consuming fire". We cannot truly live without Him, and yet, when we have Him, let us not think that He can be tamed or stifled by us.

The Fire *Then*

As the *outside element* in the equation, the fire was what came down after everything else was in place, causing the sacrifice to be consumed. Without this consumption, this sign of acceptance, the sacrifice wasn't really a sacrifice; and the Israelites were no different from the idol-worshipping nations around them. The Israelites were instructed never to allow the fire to go out. Keeping the flame burning was the priority that determined their entire culture and defined what it meant to be a Jew.

God commanded, *"The fire must be kept burning on the altar continuously, it must not go out"* (Lev. 6:13).

The Continual Fire

What an interesting demand God makes of Israel! He made it abundantly clear to them, repeating Himself *three times,* that the fire on the altar must be maintained day and night. He apparently wants there to be no mistake, no possibility of their being confused about what He said.

IT WAS HER PRIORITY, AND SO IT DETERMINED HER CULTURE; FOR WHATEVER WE PRIORITIZE WILL ULTIMATELY DETERMINE THE CULTURE OF OUR LIFE.

And so, Israel receives her national mandate. God is communicating clearly, with no chance of misunderstanding, the thing she is to focus on: *The flame must be kept burning.*

Think about all that this meant . . .

Someone always had to be present to maintain the fire so that the flame would never be extinguished.

Someone had to guard over the flame if there was wind or rain.

Someone had to gather massive amounts of wood for the fire to be on hand at all times.

Someone had to watch over it at night.

This work fell to the priests—a whole subset of the people of Israel whose main function now became to offer up the sacrifice; but more importantly, *to tend to the flame.* If there was going to be a priestly tribe, then there had to be provisions for them. So, laws went into effect about how the priests were to be provided for. Three times a year, as the people celebrated the Feasts, certain portions of their offerings were set aside for the priests.

In short, the national mandate of keeping the flame burning *affected the whole nation*. It was their prime directive—their absolute priority. And the implementation of this priority affected every aspect of their life.

Israel understood that the *only thing* which separated her from the nations of the world was the flame of the presence of God in her midst. This flame marked her with not only distinction, but also with privilege and responsibility. It was her priority, and so it determined her culture; for whatever we prioritize will ultimately determine the culture of our life.

IF WE DO NOT HAVE HIS PRESENCE, WE HAVE NOTHING. WE ARE JUST ANOTHER DO-GOOD SOCIAL CLUB; ANOTHER GATHERING OF PEOPLE ORGANIZED TOGETHER.

It is so interesting that the flame was not to be allowed to die out. Why was that? Why couldn't a fresh fire simply be rekindled for each offering?

The Priority of Fire

It is as though the Lord wants Israel to see that the sacrifice and the action of sacrifice, though important, was not the ultimate importance. If all the instructions were around the bringing of the sacrifice, then sacrifice would have been the national priority, and the focus would have been on what Israel was offering up to God.

However, the emphasis clearly remained the flame, which would have symbolized God's presence to them in a very strong way. After the Lord appeared to Moses in the burning bush, the idea of God as an ever-burning entity would have been deeply ingrained in their minds. This powerful aspect of the burning, constant, consuming fire; kept day and night on the altar, was what gave Israel her identity.

The Fire *Now: Thoughts for Today*

The fire represents the presence of God. If we do not have the burning flame of God's presence in the midst of our congregations, in the midst of our programs, in the midst of our songs, we have nothing. Only by making God's presence our number one priority can we live lives of meaning, offer sacrifices of worth and become the kingdom of priests we are called to be.

> *"But you are a chosen people, a royal priesthood, a holy nation, a people belonging to God, that you may declare the praises of him who called you out of darkness into his wonderful light"* (1 Pet. 2:9).

The Flame is Our Priority

I would suggest that our priority is no different today. We are still called to keep the flame of the presence of God. His presence, and His presence alone, separates and marks us as distinct from any other group or organization. If we do not have His presence, we have nothing. We are just another do-good social club; another gathering of people organized together.

The fire of His presence alone establishes our identity; not our altars or our sacrifices. And if we do not tend to the flame of His presence and make it our *ultimate priority*, we become like all the nations around us.

God has always dwelt in the midst of a people. We should not find it surprising that He required the priests to tend to the flame. He has always been about interacting with man and moving in the midst of the congregation. He is intensely personal, but He is also intensely corporate. *"Lord, You have been our dwelling place throughout all generations"* (Ps. 90:1). He inhabits the praises of His people.

Our church services and teachings cannot *only* be about helping people develop a personal relationship with God, important as this is. We must also welcome the fire of God to our corporate gatherings. God is there, waiting to be experienced, not only by the individual, but by the people of God coming in unity and welcoming His holy fire.

If Pentecost is to teach us anything, it should be that a relationship with the Holy Spirit is not just available to an individual, but that we are invited *as a community* to experience the power of the Holy Spirit.

This is not easy, and it is something that we, especially leaders, try to avoid. When God "shows up" and His fire is released, the experience may not be neat and tidy. Some people cry; some shake; some fall down; some laugh; some prophesy. Unfortunately, many sitting on the outskirts of the fire get caught up in the emotion of the moment and begin to respond in some way that is hollow and manufactured, even if it is very demonstrative. As a result, many religious people with their "God in a box" may be offended.

The fire of God released and welcomed into the corporate gathering of God's people is not easy to control. There is a delicate line between what is genuine and what is hype. This should not surprise us. Moses had to deal with this, as did Peter and Paul.

Desiring the fire of God, Israel built a golden calf. They did not understand how to enter into God's presence. Simon the magician wanted the fire without the presence of God and Paul had to sternly correct the Corinthians for abusing the fiery gifts of God in worship. In the very presence of God's power, people are tempted to opt for the gifts over the Giver, the manifestation of power over the Source of power, and the experience over the Presence.

Sadly, it seems that many leaders in the Body focus the corporate gatherings only on teaching good principles, reaching the lost or providing good programs for families. These things in themselves are not bad, *but they are not the national priority of the Kingdom of God!* These things are safe for the hidden areas of resistance in our souls, but they are not what we are called to first. The corporate and national priority we have as a people is to be *keepers of the flame,* and to offer up an acceptable sacrifice. This can only be accomplished if we receive and release the presence of God—the flame of the Lord—in a personal and corporate way.

WE MUST DISCERN WHAT IS OF HIS PRESENCE AND HOLD FAST TO IT; SHOWING PATIENCE AND LOVE TO EACH OTHER ALONG THE WAY.

It will be messy.

It will not be easy.

If it was not easy for Moses or the apostles,
why do we think it will be easy for us?

But if we are to be a holy nation and a royal priesthood, we must understand that everything we hear in Scripture is not only about learning principles and applying intellectual knowledge, as important and vital as they are. Everything we see in Scripture tells us that God wants to dwell in the midst of the community of faith. That requires the courage to let God come and *be God* in our midst.

And He chooses, almost always, to reveal Himself through weak and fallen people. We must discern what is of His presence and hold fast to it; showing patience and love to each other along the way.

We must never give up maintaining the flame . . .

Even if wildfire breaks out

even if our pride and orderly plans get burnt

even if our personal plans and agenda must be consumed

even if others withdraw from the flame and thus from us.

Keepers of the flame vigilantly keep the flame burning no matter what!

CHAPTER 14

THE FIRE OF THE FEAR OF THE LORD

"Therefore, since we are receiving a kingdom that cannot be shaken,
let us be thankful, and so worship God acceptably
with reverence and awe, for our 'God is a consuming fire.'"
HEBREWS 12:28-29

A God who is not terrifying is no God at all.

We live in an age in which we seem to be reducing God to the lowest common denominator; minimizing Him to some kind of glorified greeting card sentiment. God has become in popular culture synonymous with good feelings and pithy expressions like, "Forgive yourself" and, "How can you love others if you don't first love yourself?" Pop theology equates feeling good with feeling God.

Keepers of the flame build the altar, bring the sacrifice and maintain the fire. That fire isn't just fed by the believer's passion. Fire comes from the very throne and person of God (Dan. 7:9, Heb. 12:29).

The God of the Bible does not show Himself to be a god of pop culture.

He is . . .
Great

Terrible

Awesome

Almighty

Demanding

Relentless

Fierce

Overpowering

The Lion of the tribe of Judah.

He rides on the wind and speaks in the thunder and writes with the lightning. He kills the firstborn of all Egypt, demands the slaughter of the Amalekites and turns a king into a madman for seven years.

In fact, the wisest place to begin in life, we are told, is by fearing the Lord. Here is just a sampling of scriptural injunctions to embrace the fear of the Lord:

Ps. 111:10: *"The fear of the LORD is the beginning of wisdom; all who follow his precepts have good understanding. To him belongs eternal praise."*

Prov. 1:7: *"The fear of the Lord is the beginning of knowledge, but fools despise wisdom and discipline."*

Prov. 2:5: *"Then you will understand the fear of the LORD, And find the knowledge of God."*

Prov 9:10: *"The fear of the LORD is the beginning of wisdom, And the knowledge of the Holy one is understanding."*

Prov. 15:33: *"The fear of the* LORD *teaches a man wisdom, and humility comes before honor."*

Prov. 19:23: *"The fear of the* LORD *leads to life: Then one rests content, untouched by trouble.."*

Prov. 22:4: *"Humility and the fear of the* LORD *bring wealth and honor and life."*

Isa. 33:6: *"He will be the sure foundation for your times, a rich store of salvation and wisdom and knowledge; the fear of the* LORD *is the key to this treasure."*

2 Cor. 7:1: *"Therefore, having these promises, beloved, let us cleanse ourselves from all filthiness of the flesh and spirit, perfecting holiness in the fear of God (NKJV)."*

Eph 5:21: *". . . submitting to one another in the fear of God (NKJV)."*

We are conditioned in the American Christian Church to believe that all of those attributes of God so evident in the Old Testament have somehow vanished now that we are in the "age of grace."

We are tempted to make the faulty assumption that God's severe justice applies to everyone but us. We may even find ourselves having a misguided mindset such as this:

"God was apparently quite violent and ill-tempered in the revelation of Him in the Old Testament, and He plans on demonstrating Himself as quite furious with the planet at the end of age—the last days—which are drawing very near, when He will once again throw upon the earth all kinds of plagues and pestilences and other drastic inconveniences. But for now, as the American Christian Church, we have managed to live in this in-between age of grace and to be spared all that was and is to come."

Interesting, isn't it? How convenient for us.

There is of course, something far more terrifying than the displeasure of God. There is something more disquieting, frightening and undoing than His rebuke. Do we know what it is?

His absence.

God is, of course, omnipresent. All of creation is sustained and maintained by His Word. God's absence refers to the withdrawal of His favor and response. In His absence, we experience a wilderness of silence and desperation. When He hides His face, we long for His touch. We cry out with the psalmist:

> *Do not hide Your face from me;*
> *Do not turn Your servant away in anger;*
> *You have been my help;*
> *Do not leave me nor forsake me,*
> *O God of my salvation*
> (Ps. 27:9 NKJV).

> *O God, do not keep silent;*
> *be not quiet, O God, be not still*
> (Ps. 83:1).

We may feel that God is silent when we are being disciplined by Him. If we are being corrected by God, at least He is still dealing with us! For the final goal of all His dealing is always our good, our prosperity and our full blessing. Like any good parent, His discipline comes when we are not measuring up to our full potential, and therefore setting ourselves up for failure and disappointment.

Something awful happens when God absents Himself from us. When He simply leaves and Ichabod is written over the doorposts of a person, family or group, what hope is there then?

Is it possible for Him to leave without our knowing it?

Is it possible for Him to remove His presence from His people and for them to continually role-play worship and relationship?

How long must God withdraw before we are awestruck by fear?

When God Withdraws

In 1 Samuel 2, we read the tragic story of the sons of Eli, the High Priest. The religious system of the day was in full swing. People were bringing their sacrifices regularly to the priests to offer up to the Lord as required, but the priests were not treating the sacrifices properly. The sons of the High Priest were exploiting the people and using their position as a means of fleshly self gratification; rather than realizing that their call as servants of God was to be just that—servants.

Apparently, in response to the continued sin, God's presence (perhaps most often discernible by His voice) had been withdrawing for some time. 1 Sam. 3:1 reports, *"In those days the word of the Lord was rare; there were not many visions."* Can there be any doubt that the rarity of the word of the Lord was in direct response to the continued exercise of dead religion without true repentance?

The Lord finds fault not only with Hophni and Phineas—the young, brash, sinful priests; but also with Eli, their older father. Why?

Because Eli, while not condoning his sons' sin, and even calling for them to stop, *still allowed the system they were propagating to bring increase and security to him.*

"Why do you honor your sons more than me by fattening yourselves on the choice part of every offering made by the people of Israel?" (1 Samuel 2:29b). Eli wanted his sons to change, but he enjoyed the fruit of their sin just the same.

The priestly family of Eli relied on two things which caused them to be lulled into complacency and to lose the fear of the Lord. First, there had been many prophetic promises that had been spoken over their family line regarding their ministry before the Lord (1 Sam. 2:30). Secondly, they were relying on the name of their position. After all, they were the priests of the Lord! Their position was honored by the people, even though there was a general sense that something was not right about the state of the religious system.

TOMORROW, GOD CAN RAISE UP A WHOLE NEW GENERATION OF BELIEVERS WHO WILL RUN HIS HOUSE IN HIS WAY IF WE DO NOT CONDUCT OUR AFFAIRS WITH THE FEAR OF THE LORD AS OUR STANDARD.

How often we rely on past promises and our lofty religious positions to protect us from the anger of the Lord!

How easy it is to rationalize away the voice that calls us to holiness and unpopular decisions!

I have often heard, and I myself have preached the famous line, "God's plan for the world is the Church. He has no plan B. He will use us and bring His Kingdom through His people, the Church."

I understand the sentiment being expressed here, but isn't it possible that this has led to a kind of proud, subconscious false security?

Jesus said, "*. . . I will build my Church and the gates of Hades will not overcome it*" (Matt. 16:18b), but do we remember that it is *His* Church, not ours, that He is building? Do we really think that just because the word "Jesus" or "Christian" or "Evangelical" or "Spirit-filled" is on our letterhead, this obligates God to validate what we do?

Jesus said to the Pharisees, *"I tell you that out of these stones God can raise up children for Abraham"* (Matt. 3:9). In the same way today, we must understand that inclusion in the plan and presence of God is not our guaranteed right because of some prayer we prayed fifteen years ago, or because we call ourselves Christians.

Tomorrow, God can raise up a whole new generation of believers who will run His house in His way if we do not conduct our affairs with the fear of the Lord as our standard. If there is anything we see from the whole council of Scripture, it is that God is not obligated to our religious systems. He will work with us, correct us, beckon us, draw us and discipline us. But in the end, if we heed not, He will simply withdraw from us.

Gradually, we are left only with the outer shell—the traditions, the phrases, the activities, the songs and the systems . . . .but He has silenced His voice and withdrawn His favor.

However, God does not leave Himself without a witness (Acts 14:17). As in the days of Eli, God will always seek out a remnant.

Even now, He is out walking in the night, whispering to Samuel, *one who will listen and obey his voice; one who will become a keeper of the flame.*

Keepers of the flame draw near to the fire of the altar in the fear of the Lord. That fear prompts them to repentance, purity and holiness. Without that fear, they encounter only the silence of God.

Draw near to His consuming fire. Let every impurity be burned away so that nothing hinders His voice, His face or His presence.

CHAPTER 15

THE FIRE OF OVERWHELMING PRESENCE

*As he neared Damascus on his journey, suddenly a light from heaven
flashed around him. He fell to the ground and heard a voice say to him,
"Saul, Saul, why do you persecute me?"*

ACTS 9:3-4

Experiencing God is a bit like a rollercoaster; only without the safety bars.

To truly walk with God and discover His presence, we must reconcile ourselves to the challenge of daily surprises and moment by moment changes.

In Isaiah 43:18-21 NKJV, God declares,

*"Do not remember the former things,
Nor consider the things of old.
Behold, I will do a new thing,
Now it shall spring forth;
Shall you not know it?
I will even make a road in the wilderness
And rivers in the desert.*

The beast of the field will honor Me,
The jackals and the ostriches,
Because I give waters in the wilderness
And rivers in the desert,
To give drink to My people, My chosen.

This people I have formed for Myself;
They shall declare My praise."

The word *new* in this context implies *change*. As God unfolds His plan in our lives, we continually experience something of God and of life that we have never before encountered. The old things of God that we have grasped give way to deeper, fresher and changing paradigms. If we idolize the old, we box God out of our lives. God refuses to live in the boxes we create for Him. As J.B. Phillips warned, "Your God is too small."

You cannot hold God in your mind any more than you can hold oil in your hand. For the minute you have figured Him out, outlined Him and systematized Him, He is no longer God.

In fact, you have just made an idol.

You don't know how to build a rollercoaster. You can't explain it.

THE MINUTE YOU HAVE FIGURED HIM OUT, OUTLINED HIM AND SYSTEMATIZED HIM, HE IS NO LONGER GOD.

You don't have a technical diagram of a rollercoaster next to your bed that you consult on a daily basis.

But *wow*, you can KNOW a rollercoaster; you can EXPERIENCE it.

Recall the waiting in line, giddy with anticipation, made more enjoyable by going with friends. Finally coming to the platform, you look at the group going just before you being strapped in, faces gleaming with excitement, with the occasional nervous looking mother wondering how she got talked into this. They launch that group, and yours moves into position to wait. In just a few minutes, the rush of air plummets your face as the train comes back into the gate.

You step into your seat, strap your self in and push on the safety bar a few times to be sure it's really locked tight. And then, finally, the jerk as the train engages and takes off ever so slowly from the gate.

Should I go on? There is the excruciatingly slow journey up to the base of the initial hill, and then the fantastic climb to the top. The glance at your friend in the next seat brings a knot to your throat as you summit. The final grip on the safety bar signals to your brain that a surge of adrenaline is about to release. And then . . . the bottom drops out!

The experience cannot be transferred. Vicarious roller coaster rides never compare to the real thing. In the same way, experiencing God at the altar, bringing the sacrifice and feeling the heat of the flame cannot be done for you. You must be there yourself to experience the fire yourself!

The Fire Must Be Encountered

It has been said that the definition of religion is people without an experience with God telling other people without an experience with God about all the people who HAD an experience with God.

If we are to be *keepers of the flame,* we must know that the flame is to be felt. God is to be experienced. **The fire of God will not be kept at safe distance through the building of theological or cultural barriers that protect the comfort zone of our religious culture.**

There is nothing in Scripture that tells us that God is anything less than an aggressive invader who demands all or nothing, hot or cold. The confrontation in His flame presents a choice: *"Choose for yourselves this day whom you will serve"* (Josh.24:15a).

Fire Radically Impassions Us

Can we really claim that the Holy Spirit is a gentleman? He came as a rushing mighty wind, and those upon whom he rested brought upheaval to every city and town they went to!

Now, I can hear already the standard reply, "Well, Brother Robert, we have to have balance. The important thing is to be balanced!"

Could someone show me ANYWHERE in Scripture ANYONE who was considered BALANCED?

Was Abraham BALANCED when he abandoned all and followed a voice into a new land?

Was Gideon BALANCED when he forsook the strength of a mighty army for a rabble band of untrained men?

Was it a BALANCED decision for David to fight Goliath, or for Shadrach, Meshach and Abednego to disobey the King?

Was Jael BALANCED as she plunged the tent peg into the skull of Sisera?

Was Ezekiel BALANCED as he lay naked on his side for 390 days?

Was JESUS BALANCED when He let his parents leave and stayed in the temple as a young boy? When he called a tax collector, the lowlife of His day, to be His disciple? When he had a conversation with the prostitute at the well? When he railed against the Pharisees?

When He went willingly, silently, to the cross?

It seems to me that it is very easy to use the word *balanced* to justify mediocrity, apathy and lukewarmness.

Perhaps the best way to be truly balanced is to be radical in all directions equally at the same time; to go beyond living only from finite principles to living in response to divine insight.

Who was more loving and merciful than Jesus? Yet who was more confrontational? He was patient with his ever-failing disciples, but seemed to give the rich young ruler only one chance to make the right decision.

Paul, at one point in his ministry, allows himself to be lowered in a basket to flee for his life: self-protection. But at another time, he ignores the prophetic warning of Agabus that he will be bound and killed if he goes to Rome: self-sacrifice.

The point is that if we have God locked in a box, living solely on principles derived from our limited viewpoint, we may be able to justify our behavior (even scripturally) but still miss the heart of God in a matter.

A Daily Desperation

God is not a distant idea to soothe the soul into a place of constant gray.

Have we confused numbness with peace?

Could it be that the thing defining spiritual greatness in the giants of Scripture—Moses, David, Jesus, Paul—was not that they focused only on the fact that they had "found" God, but that they were also driven by a daily, desperate pursuit of Him?

Out of desperation, Moses asked to see the very fire that could consume him, "Please, show me Your glory" (Ex. 33:18 NKJV). No man can see God and live. That's so true. We must die to ourselves and our banal existence in order to experience true life in Christ. The old is consumed by fire . . . the new is ablaze with the fire of the light of Christ. Moses was unbalanced, radical, impassioned and desperate for God.

Out of desperation, David cried out,

One thing I have desired of the LORD, That will I seek:
That I may dwell in the house of the LORD
All the days of my life,
To behold the beauty of the LORD,
And to inquire in His temple (Ps. 27:4 NKJV).

David could have desired power and riches, but he chose God's presence. Nothing in David's life went right unless it was first birthed in God's presence. Yes, it seemed unbalanced for David to fight a bear, lion and giant. It was unbalanced to oppose the Philistines. But David had found a supernatural source of strength and courage beyond the commonplace arena of daily life and empty ritual. In the house of the Lord, experiencing His beauty and presence, David had become unbalanced, radical, impassioned and desperate for God.

DAVID HAD FOUND A SUPERNATURAL SOURCE OF STRENGTH AND COURAGE BEYOND THE COMMONPLACE ARENA OF DAILY LIFE AND EMPTY RITUAL.

Jesus demonstrated radical obedience by doing only what the Father showed Him to do, *"Most assuredly, I say to you, the Son can do nothing of Himself, but what He sees the Father do; for whatever He does, the Son also does in like manner"* (John 5:19 NKJV). So Jesus was unbalanced, radical, impassioned and desperate for God.

Paul cries out, *"that I may know Him and the power of His resurrection, and the fellowship of His sufferings, being conformed to His death"* (Phil. 3:10 NKJV). Paul had religious prestige and power, education, status and position. Yet, he gives it all up, calling it dung, so that he might become unbalanced, radical, impassioned and desperate for God.

I am not saying that our search after God should be focused on the pursuit of supernatural or mystical experiences. The experience in and of itself has no value or ability to satisfy.

In a very real way, we must understand that everything we know about the manifest presence of God, from Scripture and from Church history, tells us that His presence is not comfortable.

Whether it is the crying out from revelations of hell through the preaching of Jonathan Edwards, or the trembling of the Shakers and the Quakers, or the excessive volume and emotional display of Count Zinzendorf and the Moravians, or the laughing and shaking of today's revival movements, God's manifest presence is OVER-WHELMING to the human psyche. Whatever our response is—laughing, crying, shaking, falling, extraordinary stillness—be sure that God is to be EXPERIENCED.

Offering an awesome God

We are not selling second hand revelation. We are not selling bottled water. We are offering LIVING WATER that flows in the river of the life of God, which emanates from His throne. And this generation is desperately thirsty for a taste of the real thing. They are hungry and thirsty for a spiritual experience with God. They will not be satisfied with a flannel graph Jesus. They are looking for the tangible intangible. And we must offer Him to them.

THIS GENERATION EITHER WALLOWS IN LIFELESS MATERIALISM AND DISTRACTION, OR WORSE, IS TURN-ING TO THE FALSE GODS OF THE NEW AGE OR ISLAM BECAUSE WE AS BELIEVERS HAVE NOT SHOWN THEM THE GOD WHO WILL CAUSE THEIR BLOOD TO BOIL AND THEIR HEART TO SING.

That, of course, is not safe. It is not neat or structured. It doesn't necessarily fit into our ninety-minute Sunday morning time frame that fits within the comfort zone of the nominal Church-goer. Again, there are no safety bars here. No way to get around it. We can't rationalize the need for a passionate experience of God away, or hope that it will disappear in the distraction of this year's Easter cantata.

Seeking God's presence, this genera-tion shows up with demons to be cast out, deep hurts to be healed, chains to be broken and freedom to be declared. A generation sits enslaved in horrible bondage. Society is dismantling in front of our very eyes. And whose fault is it? Washington's? The school systems? Hollywood's?

No. This generation either wallows in lifeless materialism and distraction, or worse, is turning to the false gods of the New Age or Islam because *we as believers* have not shown them the God who will cause their blood to boil and their heart to sing. We have offered the lowest common denominator of Christianity, (which doesn't even resemble the biblical picture of the word) because our "God in a box" draws the biggest crowds and brings in the largest offerings. We have not shown the God worthy of sacrifice, of battle and of passionate love.

If we are to offer this generation authentic spirituality, and allow them to be disciples of Jesus, then we must offer them all He is. We must offer the standard of the *daily* cross, the *daily* baptism, the *daily* rushing, mighty wind and the *daily* tongues of fire. We must make offerings as costly as the shipwrecks of Paul, the civil disobedience of Daniel, the miracles of Peter and the death-defying courage of Esther.

We must once again wrestle with God.

CHAPTER 16

THE FIRE
OF REVELATION

"Is not My word like fire?" declares the LORD,
"and like a hammer which shatters a rock?"

JEREMIAH 23:29 NASB

An ancient Jewish Midrash asks something like this, "Was Abram the first one that God called or the first that heard and obeyed the call?"

The omnipresent God constantly reveals Himself. He speaks through creation, dreams, mighty acts in history, prophets, visions and many other ways. But who will listen? Who will obey?

The LORD had said to Abram,

> *"Leave your country, your people and your father's household and*
> *go to the land I will show you. I will make you into a great*
> *nation and I will bless you;*
> *I will make your name great, and you will be a blessing.*
> *I will bless those who bless you, and whoever curses you I will curse;*
> *and all peoples on earth will be blessed through you."*
> *So Abram left, as the LORD had told him . . .* (Gen. 12:1-4a).

The Lord spoke. In the midst of towering ziggurats beckoning him to worship false gods and without the benefit of scriptures, tradition or prior religious experience, Abram heard an unfamiliar, unseen voice calling him to do that which was unthinkable, unimaginable, nontraditional and radically new. A voice he believed to be the voice of God, demanded him to do what he had never done, to go where he had never been and to receive a promise that he would never personally experience.

Calling You

How would you have responded? A voice in the night beckons you to step into a new season without any prior context for understanding. Would you think it simply your own thoughts prompting you to do something irrational?

To whom could you turn for confirmation or support? Certainly your family would not want to leave the comfortable for the uncomfortable, the familiar for the unfamiliar and the known for the unknown.

All relatives must go with you or be abandoned.

All prior religious understandings written in stones and on the faces of idols must be rejected for that which is invisible and beyond understanding.

Would you obey?

Would you dare keep burning such an awesome, mysterious, uncontrollable flame?

"The Lord spoke." Even more strongly, "The Lord commanded."

The call to go came without explanation, only promise.

The call to follow a voice and constantly keep a flame of faith ablaze was not accompanied by visible manifestations, signs and wonders.

No one trembled or fell in the Spirit.

No one sang a prophetic song.

No one gave a word of knowledge accompanied by two or more witnessing, confirming interpretations.

No one heard the voice but you.

No one could be blamed for the consequences of obedience or disobedience but you.

No one was called to keep the flame but you. What if you had been Abram and heard such a voice. Would you have paid the price and made the sacrifice of obedience?

Fiery Words

We are believers. We are those who have a real faith that God exists, and that He is actively involved in bringing about His purposes in the earth today. We have every reason to believe that the God of the Bible, the God who spoke to Abram, is the God of today; and that salvation history is still being accomplished in our generation. He is still moving, still calling, still performing miracles and, most definitely, still speaking.

Some may ask, "Is God speaking to humanity today as He did to the ancients—the patriarchs, prophets, priests, apostles and kings?

> *Then I said, "I will not make mention of Him,*
> *Nor speak anymore in His name."*
> *But His word was in my heart like a burning fire*
> *Shut up in my bones;*
> *I was weary of holding it back,*
> *And I could not*
> (Jer. 20:9 NKJV).

I don't think the question is really whether or not God continues to speak to us. The question we must ask ourselves is, "Are we listening?"

And to ask that really implies much more. To listen and not obey actually denotes that we are not really listening at all. Throughout the Torah, God says over and over again, *"If you carefully obey the voice of the Lord . . . "* (cf. Ex. 5:2, 23:21f, Dt. 4:30, 13:4, 15:15, 27:10).

Are we listening to Him and obeying His voice?

I DON'T THINK THE QUESTION IS REALLY WHETHER OR NOT GOD CONTINUES TO SPEAK TO US. THE QUESTION WE MUST ASK OURSELVES IS, "ARE WE LISTENING?"

Hearing, Obeying and Being Changed

All kinds of reasons exist as to why we might not want to hear and obey the voice of God—ignorance, sin, doubt, pain, rebellion, fear. I believe the chief of these is fear.

When God speaks and you receive and obey, His fiery word melts you, molds you and changes you. Permanently. To live with a God who speaks with you regularly demands that you be in the place of being open to daily change. And, fundamentally, humans don't like change.

Change is uncomfortable, unpredictable and uncontrollable. We often fear change.

So, we prefer deafness to transition.

We prefer houses to tents.

We prefer destinations to journeys.

If there is one thing that the voice of God does, *it moves us.* From His words to Abram, "Get up and go!" to the words of Jesus, "Go ye into all the world!" the primary result of the word of God in the life of believers seems to be motion.

Blessed are those whose strength is in you,
who have set their hearts on pilgrimage.
As they pass through the Valley of Baca,
they make it a place of springs;
the autumn rains also cover it with pools.
They go from strength to strength,
till each appears before God in Zion
(Ps. 84:5-7).

To open your heart to the voice of God is to open your heart to hope. Reinhold Niebuhr once remarked that, "Faith is a citadel of hope built on the brink of despair." And that is a scary thing.

Hope moves us to the edge of our strength, knowing that when we are weak, He is strong.

Hope moves us from the brink of our courage to face the realm of risk and unpredictability.

Hope moves us to the precipice of the visible, forcing us to see the invisible, hear the incredible and do the impossible with God's hope instead of in our own confidence; so that we live in a new realm.

HOPE MOVES US TO THE PRECIPICE OF THE VISIBLE, FORCING US TO SEE THE INVISIBLE, HEAR THE INCREDIBLE AND DO THE IMPOSSIBLE WITH GOD'S HOPE INSTEAD OF IN OUR OWN CONFIDENCE; SO THAT WE LIVE IN A NEW REALM.

Now faith is the substance of things hoped for, the evidence of things not seen. For by it the elders obtained a good testimony. By faith we understand that the worlds were framed by the word of God, so that the things which are seen were not made of things which are visible (Hebrews 11:1-3 NKJV).

To hope is to put at risk all we are and have in exchange for all

He is and provides. Such risk is scary and prompts most people to choose to live without hope. They may say they hope for things, but it is not a deep, risk-taking hope.

Rather, they spend their lives building walls of self-protection. This is usually the self-protection of cynicism, which lives with an expectation that things will not go well; that the world is meaningless, so we must prepare for the worst. Sometimes people live in the self-protection of denial, which strives to build up a perfect little fortified world and ignore the reality that lurks outside those walls.

> WE MUST SEE THE REALITY OF THE WORLD AS IT IS, BUT ALSO THE REALITY OF THE WORLD AS GOD WANTS IT TO BE.

But to live with God-given hope demands great courage. It means that we must see the reality of the world as it is, but also the reality of the world as God wants it to be. We must recognize the battle between those two realities. And then, we must get involved.

The Flame Consumes Inertia and Ignites Motion

God continually prodded Israel to go to the land He would show them. Are you ready for motion and the resulting responsibility?

Fiery hope incinerates past baggage and constraints. To move ahead, we must get rid of excess baggage including negative, sarcastic and cynical companions who try to drive while gazing into the rear view mirror. God's fiery hope consumes past guilt, failure and sin. God demands, *"Do not remember the former things, nor consider the things of old"* (Isaiah 43:18 NKJV). Hope has us discard the old wineskins for the new!

The flame of hope demands a journey. It may not be a geographic journey, but hope requires that we embark on a life that is a long adventure, ultimately moving us from man's hell toward God's heaven. It's a journey of change, transforming us from faith to faith, hope to hope and glory to glory. The option to stop or turn back does not exist. We cannot give up; we cannot quit!

And many times, the reality of what we *see* around us is so radically different than what we *hear* God saying, that we are tempted to decide that the voice of God is really just our own imaginations. But there is no authority in wishing, no demand in our sentiments. Those things are negotiable and deniable. So we retreat into the gray world of safety, deciding to ignore the voice, because His hope is too costly—too black and white.

The Tests of Fiery Revelation

Revelation tests us. The voice of God tests us—individually and corporately.

What did God say?

How do we know it was Him?

Did He say how and when He was going to act, or just what He was going to do?

What must we do to obey?

The issues raised the minute you confront the reality of the fire of revelation are so problematic, so messy, so emotionally-entangling and difficult that many of us retreat to the safety of a God who has been mute for 2000 years. We adopt principles over presence. Like the children of Israel, we prefer others to hear God for us.

> *When the people saw the thunder and lightning and heard the trumpet and saw the mountain in smoke, they trembled with fear. They stayed at a distance and said to Moses, "Speak to us yourself and we will listen. But do not have God speak to us or we will die." Moses said to the people, "Do not be afraid. God has come to test you, so that the fear of God will be with you to keep you*

from sinning." The people remained at a distance, while Moses approached the thick darkness where God was (Ex. 20:18-21).

Moses approached the thick darkness where God was. How interesting. We always think of God in terms of light, and yet here He is, speaking in the darkness.

As individuals, as families, as congregations, as the regional body of Christ in this day, we must begin to hear and understand what God is saying. We must begin to grapple with the reality of the voice of God. As ill equipped as we seem to be to hear and obey, we must try.

Without His voice, what hope is there for the earth, or for our lives? Hope creates within us the confident expectation that we will hear God's voice and be empowered by His Spirit to obey whatever word He speaks. The psalmist sings of this truth:

> *You are my hiding place and my shield; I **hope** in Your **word**.*
> *Depart from me, you evildoers,*
> *For **I will keep the commandments** of my God!*
> *Uphold me according to Your **word**, that I may live;*
> *And do not let me be ashamed of my **hope***
> (Psalm 119:114-116 NKJV, emphasis added).

His voice . . .

      Creates

                              Guides

                Protects

                                Comforts

      Leads

                                    Confirms

                        Appoints

            Dismantles

                            Establishes.

The price for hearing His voice is that we must begin to hope in His word. To do that while living in the context of worldly influences and temptations is not easy, popular or comfortable. But the word of the Lord must be recaptured by our generation, *lest we live with the curse of its absence.* There are generations who lived without His voice and experienced all of the negative, destructive impact that must be endured when heavenly vision is scarce, as in the days of Eli.

When revelation comes to us, we are tested by it in so many ways. Having received a gem of revelation from God . . .

Does it puff us up?

Do we feel better than others because we have sensed God's voice?

Do we receive the word of the Lord as it is, or do we color it with out own un-broken human desires and wants?

Do we try to manipulate the word to accomplish some hidden agenda of our own?

Do we automatically sense the right to share this word, or are we open to being like Mary who, receiving the word of the Lord, simply *pondered these things in her heart?*

Are we open to being WRONG? Can we admit our mistakes openly and pub-licly ask for forgiveness?

Are we firmly aware that we "see in part" and that no matter how mature we may think ourselves in the Lord, He has established that no one sees the full picture?

Does the word of the Lord lead us to hearts of judgment, or hearts of mercy?

THE PRICE FOR HEARING HIS VOICE IS THAT WE MUST BEGIN TO HOPE IN HIS WORD. TO DO THAT WHILE LIVING IN THE CONTEXT OF WORLDLY INFLUENCES AND TEMPTATIONS IS NOT EASY. BUT THE WORD OF THE LORD MUST BE RECAPTURED BY OUR GENERATION, LEST WE LIVE WITH THE CURSE OF ITS ABSENCE.

Are we willing to wait for the Lord to perform His word no matter how long it takes?

God's Sovereign Timing

A friend of mine, a pastor of a large and successful church, shared with me his interesting experience with the voice of the Lord.

Thirty years earlier, while in Bible college, he had had a very specific dream in which he felt the Lord directing him to approach a certain individual, whom he sensed in the dream was in great crisis. He was to offer this individual strength and encouragement and to help him in some very specific ways.

He went to this person and shared this sense of God's leading with him. The person looked at him like he was crazy and said that he had no need of this person's help or relationship. My friend felt embarrassed and ashamed and was sure that he had been completely mistaken.

Twenty-eight years later, my friend received a phone call from this same person. The person was in trouble, with some very specific situations, which matched exactly my friend's dream almost three decades earlier. This troubled person had forgotten the word the Lord had spoken twenty-eight years before. However, my friend remembered it vividly and was able to reach out to him in care, love and compassion as God used him to minister to this troubled soul in a great crisis.

Why had twenty-eight years needed to pass? Why did my friend have to endure the shame of the earlier reproof when his offer of help was rejected?

We do not have to understand all the ways in which God's voice works to believe that His voice is real and that we can trust Him. It's important to follow God's process for hearing and obeying His word.

1. **Know the Word.** We must earnestly study the Scriptural principles for knowing and following the voice of God.
2. **Be in godly, holy relationships.** We must be part of a solid, intimate community of faith, which can help us discern and understand the process of God's word in our lives. We love and care for one another, speaking the truth in love, as we walk by faith and obedience.
3. **Cultivate humility.** We must be open to the very real possibility that we can make mistakes. We must humbly admit when we are wrong. In being open and transparent, we know that the possibility exists that when we think we hear the voice of God, it may be our own desires, thoughts or a voice of confusion. We must be willing to lay things down and receive the whole counsel of God from the authority of Scripture, and the Spiritual authority of the pastors and believers God puts in our lives.
4. **Walk in faith.** We must keep believing and trusting, even when we don't understand or see the fullness of the promise released in exactly the time and way we think it will be. If God said it, don't give up . . . don't quit . . . keep praying . . . be persistent and steadfast . . . stand firm.

Time Reveals Faith

Do you remember the promise to Abram? *"He [God] took him [Abram] outside and said, 'Look up at the heavens and count the stars— if indeed you can count them.'"* Then He said to him, *"'So shall your off- spring be.' Abram believed the LORD, and he credited it to him as right- eousness"* (Gen. 15:5-6).

Abram, renamed *Abraham*—father of nations, believed the word of the Lord. But at the end of his life what did he have to demonstrate

PERHAPS WHEN
ABRAM FIRST HEARD
THIS PROMISE,
HE EXPECTED A
DIFFERENT, MORE
FULLY-REALIZED
MANIFESTATION.
BUT IN THE END,
HE SAW THROUGH
EYES OF FAITH THAT
HIS SEED, ISAAC,
WOULD PRODUCE
THE FULL MEASURE OF
GOD'S PROMISE.

in the natural realm the reality of that word? Only Isaac; just a seed.

Perhaps when Abram first heard this promise, he expected a different, more fully-realized manifestation—a different timing, a greater amount of children. But in the end, he saw through eyes of faith that his seed, Isaac, would produce the full measure of God's promise.

Today, you and I are continuing the fulfillment of that promise. We are sons and daughters of Abraham in faith. The seed is still bearing fruit.

Hope is kept alive in the earth by those brave hearts, *keepers of the flame,* who believe in God's dream for this planet; not in a vague sentimental way, but in an immediate and personal way.

We must listen.

We must believe.

We must love and obey.

We must hope.

Now abideth these three—faith, hope and love. Such fuel the flame of revelation.

CHAPTER 16

THE FIRE OF PERSEVERANCE

*"Only hold on to what you have until I come. To him who overcomes
and does my will to the end, I will give authority over the nations—
'He will rule them with an iron scepter; he will dash them to pieces like
pottery'—just as I have received authority from my Father.
I will also give him the morning star."*

REVELATION 2:25-28

*Therefore, having been justified by faith, we have peace with God
through our Lord Jesus Christ, through whom also we have access
by faith into this grace in which we stand, and rejoice in hope of
the glory of God. And not only that, but we also glory in tribulations, knowing that tribulation produces perseverance; and perseverance, character; and character, hope. Now hope does not dis-
appoint, because the love of God has been poured out in our hearts
by the Holy Spirit who was given to us* (Rom. 5:1-5 NKJV).

Without perseverance, hope is extinguished. Perseverance runs
the race to the finish line as we execute our part to see the fullness of
the promise released. If we are to be *keepers of the flame* who see the
Lord's acceptable sacrifice lifted up in a way that moves heaven and

earth, then we need to be willing to be a part of God's answer, God's solution to the needs around us.

We need to become *"doers of the word"* (James 1:22 NKJV), adding action to our faith. When we see the great chasm between the world as it is and the world as God wants it to be, it can seem overwhelming to us, and we wonder if our actions make a difference at all. It is then that we must make a *leap of faith.* That leap of faith requires believing that seemingly insignificant and sometimes even hidden actions of obedience are bright bursts of light that, however momentarily, overcome the darkness. In that moment of obedience and hidden victory, the Kingdom of God has triumphed over darkness. Faith augmented by action and kept alive by perseverance *does* make a difference.

THAT LEAP OF FAITH REQUIRES BELIEVING THAT SEEMINGLY INSIGNIFICANT AND SOMETIMES EVEN HIDDEN ACTIONS OF OBEDIENCE ARE BRIGHT BURSTS OF LIGHT THAT, HOWEVER MOMENTARILY, OVERCOME THE DARKNESS.

Persistence Means Overcoming

We must train ourselves not just to gain momentary victories, but to live lives of constant perseverance, giving ourselves to the *courageous faith* that produces a life of *courageous obedience.* This is an *overcoming* lifestyle.

Keeping the flame isn't a task for the fainthearted or the easily discouraged.

Of course, the temptations to quit come frequently. Quitting may seem natural and reasonable. But by giving up on God's promise leads to aborting the vision and failing to see the fulfillment of His vision and dream for the world.

As overcomers, *keepers of the flame* persist in pushing ahead through obstacles. There is no overcoming without hurdles and tribulations. *Overcoming* is the mark of those who finish strong.

Jesus sets forth these promises to overcoming *keepers of the flame:*

He who has an ear, let him hear what the Spirit says to the churches. To him who overcomes I will give to eat from the tree of life, which is in the midst of the Paradise of God (Rev. 2:7 NKJV).

He who has an ear, let him hear what the Spirit says to the churches. He who overcomes will not be hurt at all by the second death. (Rev. 2:11).

He who has an ear, let him hear what the Spirit says to the churches. To him who overcomes I will give some of the hidden manna to eat. And I will give him a white stone, and on the stone a new name written which no one knows except him who receives it (Rev. 2:17 NKJV).

And he who overcomes, and keeps My works until the end, to him I will give power over the nations (Rev. 2:26 NKJV).

He who overcomes shall be clothed in white garments, and I will not blot out his name from the Book of Life; but I will confess his name before My Father and before His angels (Rev. 3:5 NKJV).

Him who overcomes I will make a pillar in the temple of my God. Never again will he leave it. I will write on him the name of my God and the name of the city of my God, the new Jerusalem, which is coming down out of heaven from my God; and I will also write on him my new name (Rev. 3:12).

To him who overcomes I will grant to sit with Me on My throne, as I also overcame and sat down with My Father on His throne (Rev. 3:21 NKJV).

The Apostle Paul provides an amazing example for us of long term, persevering, overcoming faith. Paul epitomizes the kind of apostolic, intercessory lifestyle needed to truly establish the Kingdom of God.

Here is a realistic, concrete description of an overcoming life . . .

> *For it seems to me that God has put us apostles on display at the end of the procession, like men condemned to die in the arena. We have been made a spectacle to the whole universe, to angels as well as to men. We are fools for Christ, but you are so wise in Christ! We are weak, but you are strong! You are honored, we are dishonored! To this very hour we go hungry and thirsty, we are in rags, we are brutally treated, we are homeless. We work hard with our own hands. When we are cursed, we bless; when we are persecuted, we endure it; when we are slandered, we answer kindly. Up to this moment we have become the scum of the earth, the refuse of the world* (1 Cor. 4:9-13).

And Paul's overcoming perseverance was not only against *outward* stresses and pressures, but also *inward* battles of the soul:

> *There was given me a thorn in my flesh, a messenger of Satan, to torment me. Three times I pleaded with the Lord to take it away from me. But he said to me, "My grace is sufficient for you, for my power is made perfect in weakness"* (2 Cor. 12:7-9a).

If we are to become *keepers of the flame,* if we are to rebuild the fallen altars and again lift up acceptable sacrifices that move the hand of heaven, then we must be prepared for a lifestyle of holy perseverance and righteous tenacity. We cannot and must not give up—not on our families, our callings, our churches, our generation, our cities and our nations.

It's easy to adopt an "end of the world" escapist mentality that resigns oneself to thinking that things are the way they are because we are in the last days. Beloved, things may be terrible in the world's systems because it is the last days, but this is no excuse for things to be lukewarm and out of order in the house of the Lord!

We are called to live lives worthy of His calling and Kingdom.

We are called to occupy until He comes, and to be a demonstration of His love to the world.

The familiar sentiment, "They will know we are Christians by our love," adjures us to remember that it is not by our large buildings, our impressive choirs, or our moralizing speeches on CNN that we will impact the world for good. The world will know we are Christians when we persevere into a corporate lifestyle worthy of the name of Christ.

Do we want to change the world?

Do we want to see His Kingdom come?

How much do we want this? What are we willing to sacrifice?

Even more so, are we willing to live overcoming LIFESTYLES of sacrifice?

The Lord is not looking for us to have a few crisis experiences of brokenness and yieldedness. He is looking for us to live lives on the altar, offered up daily to the purposes of the Kingdom of God.

A Sound in the Distance

I see in my spirit an army arising in the nations. It is an army of people dead to their reputations, to their agendas, to their own sense of self importance. They are alive unto God. Their bread is to do the will of Him who sends them.

Nothing can stop them; no outward pressure or inward pain.

Their eyes are fixed.

Their hearts are settled.

Their purpose is clear.

Their weapons are chosen.

They will not fight with worldly mindsets or understandings, but with the ancient weapons of surrender and faith. They do not contend with the world, *they overcome it.* They live and move in the Spirit as they discern and understand the will of the Lord.

Their faith is not rash or hasty. Their zeal is matched only by their wisdom. They move with great strategy. Because nothing possesses their hearts but Him, He is free to entrust all things to their care.

The persevering overcomers, called *keepers of the flame,* are at home in the offices of presidents and in the cottages of peasants, and they esteem each as important as the other as long as they are fulfilling the divine mandate.

They respond to a sound.

A sound of Majesty,
a sound of Honor,
a sound of the Voice of the Lord.

Like Elijah in 1 Kings 18, they have heard *"the sound of abundance of rain."* They have trembled at this sound. *They have let this sound permeate the depths of their being to such a place that they are now in tune with this sound, and it moves them.* Truth is their standard; love is their secret weapon.

THE WORLD WILL KNOW WE ARE CHRISTIANS WHEN WE PERSEVERE INTO A CORPORATE LIFESTYLE WORTHY OF THE NAME OF CHRIST.

They see their passion for Jesus resulting in passion for His people—hurting humanity and confused Christianity. They demonstrate their passion for Him not only in word and song, but in faithful intercessory lifestyles.

They don't just lay their lives on the altar. *They leave them there.* They persevere, daily. They fight, sweat, press through, leap over walls, run through troops, confront giants, endure hardships and are disowned by a world that doesn't understand them.

They do these things everyday.

What are you living for?

What are you giving yourself to?

What's so important that you have not joined them? Could it be that you have not yet given your all? Or, that you have not burned every bridge and crossed the point of no return?

Join their company. David is one of their generals. Esther is one of their top military strategists. Enlist today. Join the company of the perseverant. Step into the fire, the flame of overcoming perseverance.

CHAPTER 18

THE FIRE OF CONSECRATION

*I baptize you with water for repentance. But after me will come one
who is more powerful than I, whose sandals I am not fit to carry.
He will baptize you with the Holy Spirit and with fire.*

MATTHEW 3:11

What does it mean to be holy?

In holiness, we are consecrated, or set apart, solely for the Lord's
use. What does this mean?

Holiness, in Scripture, most properly
flows from an understanding of *consecration* or *being set apart*. There is, of course,
the sense of the progress of holiness in our
lives, in which we are being gradually sanctified and purified by the Lord as we continue to pursue the holiness of God in our
lives. But I want to focus, as we consider
the fire of consecration, on the understanding of being set apart *as a people* unto
the Lord.

I WANT TO FOCUS,
AS WE CONSIDER
THE FIRE OF
CONSECRATION,
ON THE
UNDERSTANDING OF
BEING SET APART
AS A PEOPLE UNTO
THE LORD.

We are crying out for the Lord to come. We are crying out for His presence. But do we realize the power and seduction of the spirit of this age, and how pervasive and invasive it is?

Do we understand how much we have been *affected* by worldly thinking and *infected* by worldly values?

We are crying out to the Lord that we would be *keepers of the flame.* We desire to follow after the tradition of the Levites who offered up acceptable sacrifices to God, which secured His blessing over Israel. We read in the Torah, *"You must distinguish between the holy and the common, between the unclean and the clean, and you must teach the Israelites all the decrees the LORD has given them through Moses"* (Lev. 10:10-11).

The Cost of Consecration

The calling of the Levites was not only to offer up an acceptable sacrifice to God, but also to be, in a sense, the national conscience of the people. They were the ones whom the Lord called to teach Israel the difference between the holy and the profane.

But do we realize the price the Levites paid to be consecrated?

The first mention of the consecration of the Levites was at the scene of the disaster of the golden calf. Aaron had allowed this idol to be built, and the children of Israel (who had just been delivered by Yahweh from Egypt) had already turned their back on Him and were pursuing the worship of idols. Moses heard this profane cacophony on the mountain, descended from the mountain and confronted the nation. Here is the scene:

> *Moses saw that the people were running wild and that Aaron had let them get out of control and so become a laughingstock to their enemies. So he stood at the entrance to the camp and said,*

"Whoever is for the LORD, come to me." And all the Levites rallied to him. Then he said to them, "This is what the LORD, the God of Israel, says: 'Each man strap a sword to his side. Go back and forth through the camp from one end to the other, each killing his brother and friend and neighbor.'" The Levites did as Moses commanded, and that day about three thousand of the people died. Then Moses said, "You have been set apart to the LORD today, for you were against your own sons and brothers, and he has blessed you this day" (Ex. 32:25-29).

What a price the Levites paid for their consecration! Can you imagine? The zeal of the Lord *consumed* them. They set their swords *against their own tribes and families* in order that the name of the Lord would not suffer further dishonor. The fear of the Lord was in them so strongly that it displaced every fear of man. There was no question about where they stood. *Wherever the Lord was, there they would be.*

Jesus mirrored this same zeal when he confronted the dead religious system of the Temple. Here is that scene:

So he made a whip out of cords, and drove all from the temple area, both sheep and cattle; he scattered the coins of the money changers and overturned their tables. To those who sold doves he said, "Get these out of here! How dare you turn my Father's house into a market!" His disciples remembered that it is written: "Zeal for your house will consume me" (John 2:15-17).

If we are to live in the fire of consecration, we must realize that zeal for our Father's House must consume us. We must have a 'no compromise mentality' with sin and strongholds, within and without. We must embrace lives that are holy in our behavior. We must then go on to embrace hearts that cry out for a standard of holiness to be raised against the things which break God's heart.

Consecration permeates and saturates everything we are: how we spend our time; how we spend our money; how we invest in relationships; how we view our day. Every moment of our time is an investment in one Kingdom or another. Are we consecrating our time, *"redeeming our time because the days are evil?"* (Eph. 5:16 NKJV).

What about the systems we are living in?

Is the peer pressure in our church communities toward righteousness or toward the standards of the world?

Are we fostering an atmosphere which encourages our teenagers to

DO THE CHILDREN IN YOUR CONGREGATION SEE MORE PEOPLE PARTICIPATING IN THE SPORTS LEAGUE OR THE PRAYER MEETING?

date as the world dates (entering prematurely into emotionally entangling relationships)? Or are we raising a Kingdom standard which lets them know there is a better way; that they should save not only their bodies but also their hearts for the one God has chosen for them?

Are we pushing a Christian music culture that *imitates* the godless forms around us; as opposed to *creating* an expression of the life of God? Are we pushing a spirit of entertainment; or are we nurturing the spirit of worship in our children?

Are we emphasizing activities like baseball leagues and roller skating nights more than our prayer meetings? Do the children in your congregation see more people participating in the sports league or the prayer meeting?

We are not *of* this world. We are not to *look* like the world, *act* like the world, *think* like the world or *be* like the world! And though hyper-religious attitudes have tried to turn that admonition into a legalism which condemns any woman who wears make-up or has short hair, or says that anyone who has a TV is probably not saved, we should not and must not resist legalism only to then settle for spiritual mediocrity. A better way exists!

Attractive Holiness

Consecration provides the way for us to live in Christ's liberty and freedom while still maintaining a passion and zeal for holiness and purity in the Lord. There is a Highway of Holiness.

> *A highway shall be there, and a road,*
> *And it shall be called the Highway of Holiness.*
> *The unclean shall not pass over it,*
> *But it shall be for others*
> *Whoever walks the road, although a fool,*
> *Shall not go astray.*
> *No lion shall be there,*
> *Nor shall any ravenous beast go up on it;*
> *It shall not be found there.*
> *But the redeemed shall walk there,*
> *And the ransomed of the LORD shall return,*
> *And come to Zion with singing,*
> *With everlasting joy on their heads.*
> *They shall obtain joy and gladness,*
> *And sorrow and sighing shall flee away*
> (Isa. 35:8-10 NKJV).

God's consecrated and dedicated Highway of Holiness is being restored and built up in this day. It is the place where holy intentions meet holy hearts and holy lifestyles, and the power and presence of God is released. Holiness is not a harsh way; it's God's way of wholeness and grace. It is the attractiveness of living life the way God intended for it to be lived.

Keepers of the flame are seen by those in and outside the Church as people whose holiness attracts people to the holiness of God. That attraction is pure and winsome; magnetic and dynamic; gracious and inviting.

The flame draws others to it with a beauty unlike anything the world tries to counterfeit. Become an attraction, not a detraction for Christ. Let your light so shine before others that they glorify God with heartfelt awe, consecrating everything they do and are to Him.

CHAPTER 19

THE FIRE OF LOVE

When I became a man, I put childish ways behind me.
Now we see but a poor reflection as in a mirror;
then we shall see face to face.
Now I know in part; then I shall know fully,
even as I am fully known.
And now these three remain: faith, hope and love.
But the greatest of these is love.

1 CORINTHIANS 13:11B-13

After having spent almost thirty years as a Christian, I am ashamed and saddened to say that I really feel I know very little about *agape* love. I understand its importance in an intellectual way. I know many things about love. But I still feel that there is something eluding me in grasping the kind of tangible meaning to the word *love*, which I believe the Lord calls us to understand and appropriate.

I know, for example, that . . .

God is love.

Faith works by love.

Greater love hath no man than this,

that he lay down his life for his friends.

God so loved.

They will know we are Christians by our love.

But somehow I feel that I can do a much better job explaining, for instance . . . hope, or trust, or faith than I can explaining love.

I have been thinking over the past few years how foundational and basic and what a priority love is in the Scripture. And yet, the vast majority of Christian literature and teaching seems to be on so many other things! I can easily think of teachers and whole ministries identified with faith, prayer, worship, deliverance, inner healing, social justice, leadership development and a host of other topics. Yet I feel that even the most elementary understanding of love escapes us in a profound way.

THE HIGHER OUR STANDARDS, THE MORE WE MUST REACH OUT IN LOVE TO THOSE WE FEEL ARE OPPOSED TO THEM.

This makes me wonder if my experience of feeling a bit at a loss when it comes to love is unique, or whether perhaps the Church needs a fresh baptism in this most foundational and necessary of all spiritual elements.

If we are to go on in Christ, we must realize that our chief purpose is to love. We must love God in word, in deed and in heart. We must love our fellow believers—not only in mental assent, or because we have a genuine affinity for someone, but intentionally. We must love the world.

If those who do not know Christ are to sense and know the love of God, it must flow from us who are His hands extended. We must love our enemies. Wow! What does THIS mean for us and how we treat those whose political and social agendas differ from our own?

Is the Church loving those whom we perceive as our enemies, or are we blasting them on CNN? I am not talking about compromising our standards, but it would seem to me that the higher our standards, the more we must reach out in love to those we feel are opposed to them.

So, it seems, there is a whole lot of loving that should be going on. And yet, what is love and how is it expressed?

Love—Feeling or Decision

My wife and I, in many ways, are very opposite. I was raised in a strict, narrow, Christian home. She was raised in a broad minded, liberal, highly intellectual Jewish home. This makes for an interesting relationship!

In the early days of our relationship, we would consistently have intense discussions (you understand what that means, don't you?) about the nature of love. Was love first a feeling, or was it first a decision?

What releases love into a situation?

Is it that the mind makes a mental decision to love, even if the emotions are frustrated at the moment? Or, does the heart consistently have to nurture and search for the feeling of love, and let the mind follow?

Which is motivational—the feeling or the decision?

Of course, with all these 'which came first, the chicken or the egg' sort of questions, there really is no comprehensive answer. It is always a blend of both and always a need to grow in whichever does not come most naturally as one matures in the process.

But we began to see that if feeling and decisions are roots, which plant themselves deep in the soil of relationship, then there is something that binds them both together—an invisible, magnetic force that keeps decisions and feelings dancing together in harmonious tension.

Love as Covenant

Keepers of the flame live in covenant love. Ultimately, feelings without decisions and decisions without feelings are both recipes for the end of love. One leads to insecurity because the heart is fickle and changeable and easily swayed in the moment. The other leads to sterility because the heart needs feelings like lungs need air. It does no good to simply say that someone is loved. The effect of love is not in the profession of the giver, but in the acceptance of the receiver.

OUR VERY RELATIONSHIP WITH GOD IS AN OUTFLOW AND FULFILLMENT OF HIS COVENANT PROMISE TO ABRAHAM. THE COVENANTS OF GOD ARE THE FRAMEWORK OF THE UNIVERSE.

Covenant is a lost concept in our day, but it must be recovered for *keepers of the flame* to move forward in reclaiming marriages, family lines, congregations, cities and generations back for the Lord. All that God is and does is through covenant.

We know Him because of covenant. Our very relationship with God is an outflow and fulfillment of His covenant promise to Abraham. Without the terms, the understanding, the reality of covenant, we have nothing. The covenants of God are the framework of the universe.

The world functions with contract relationships. And as we have learned, contracts are bound by time; covenant is eternal. Contracts demand conditions; covenant love is unconditional. Contracts expect and build in contingencies for failure; covenant love never fails. Contracts can be bilateral; covenant is always trilateral with God in the midst. Contracts are based on law and rules; covenant is based on grace and relationship. Contracts can be broken; covenant bends but doesn't break.

And so love, I am coming to understand, has everything to do with covenant. Because God loves me, He has extended an invitation to me into covenant. God has not extended an invitation merely to relationship; which He will give and take away based on my performance that day. Rather, He has offered me an unconditional covenant of love. I am His and He is mine.

I am secure in His love. I am not yet perfected into the image of Christ, but His love for me and His commitment to me are not based on my perfection.

God is love. The word does not say that God *loves*, but rather that He *is* Love. God loves me no less when I am stubborn and disobedient, and He loves me no more when I am doing well and living like I should and want to live.

LOVE IS THE INTANGIBLE, MAGNETIC FORCE THAT HOLDS ALL THINGS TOGETHER. BUT IT IS EXPRESSED IN PRACTICAL, REAL WAYS.

This is not to say that my decisions do not have consequences. Because of covenant, there are blessings and curses that I release into my life based on how I live up to the agreements of the Covenant. But these things are manifestations in the temporal world of the here and now. In the eternal world, God's love for me, His desire to bless and walk closely with me, is unconditional.

And when God does judge, or discipline, He does it with a heart of love. The judgments of the Lord are to bring us to repentance, so that covenant relationship—love relationship—can be restored. To hear many preachers preach, the judgment that is coming on the earth is something God really wants. I do not believe that the Bible demonstrates a God who delights in judgment, but rather in salvation! How great is the mercy and kindness and love of God!

Note these revealing passages about the nature of God:

"But if a wicked man turns away from all the sins he has committed and keeps all my decrees and does what is just and right,

he will surely live; he will not die. None of the offenses he has committed will be remembered against him. Because of the righteous things he has done, he will live. Do I take any pleasure in the death of the wicked?" declares the Sovereign LORD. "Rather, am I not pleased when they turn from their ways and live?" (Ezek. 18:21-23).

For God did not send his Son into the world to condemn the world, but to save the world through him (John 3:17).

If we are to release an offering, an acceptable offering, that touches the heart and moves the hand of God in this generation, then we must live in the Fire of Divine Love. Love must not be to us an abstract concept, but a *living reality.* We must seek after love, pursue love, and seek to understand the height and depth of the love of God. We must equally seek to allow this love to pour through us—not just to those whom we love easily, but to all the world, especially to those unlovely to us.

What would the world be like if we really lived in love; in covenant with God and with one another? How would things be different if all our actions were based on an honest, intentional, brave pursuit of all that is good and worthy?

The love of God and the covenant of God is not something that is abstract or ethereal. Everything we know about God, and our mandates from Scripture, tell us that our passion for Jesus must demonstrate itself in real and practical ways to our brothers and sisters in Christ and to the world around us.

Simon son of John, do you truly love me more than these?"
    "Yes, Lord," he said, "you know that I love you."
    Jesus said, "Feed my lambs."
    Again Jesus said, "Simon son of John, do you truly love me?"

He answered, "Yes, Lord, you know that I love you."

Jesus said, "Take care of my sheep."

The third time he said to him, "Simon son of John, do you love me?"

Peter was hurt because Jesus asked him the third time, "Do you love me?" He said, "Lord, you know all things; you know that I love you."

Jesus said, "Feed my sheep" (John 21:15-18a).

"Then the righteous will answer him, 'Lord, when did we see you hungry and feed you, or thirsty and give you something to drink? When did we see you a stranger and invite you in, or needing clothes and clothe you? When did we see you sick or in prison and go to visit you?'"

"The King will reply, 'I tell you the truth, whatever you did for one of the least of these brothers of mine, you did for me,'" (Matt. 25:37-40).

And so, ultimately, love is neither only feeling nor only decision, but love is covenant. Love is the intangible, magnetic force that holds all things together. But it is expressed in practical, real ways.

We must recapture love. We must recapture a real love for God and from God, which results in a real love for people. The love of God must be released to this generation. The healing stream of pure love flowing from heaven must find an outlet. It must be demonstrated. It must be maintained.

The Covenants of God compel us to give away our love, every day, in giving of our time, giving of our money, giving of our privacy, giving up of our conveniences. Self must not be on the throne of our lives. **A consumer-based Christianity which thinks that a nice, self-fulfilled American life is what Jesus came to give, must be broken through.** We must not love because it is convenient, or because we have our own self interest at heart, or because there is some return for us in it.

We must love because love is God, released to act and move and rule in the world. Love thinks about serving and caring for and giving to others. It does not seek its own.

And if love is not reciprocated? If you do not receive the expected return on your gift of love? What then?

Well, was your love conditional? And to whom, ultimately, was it directed? Ultimately, if our love is directed to and given to God, then we have received our reward. We have loved Him.

Keepers of the flame have offered up the fire of love, not in easy ways like singing songs or praying prayers or giving a few dollars. But we have offered up something that has cost us, something that has burned us. Such pleases God.

THE AROMA

*But thanks be to God, who always leads us
in triumphal procession in Christ
and through us spreads everywhere the fragrance
of the knowledge of him. For we are to God
the aroma of Christ among those who
are being saved and those who are perishing.
To the one we are the smell of death;
to the other, the fragrance of life.*

II CORINTHIANS 2:14-16A

CHAPTER 20

WE ARE
THE FRAGRANCE
OF CHRIST

We have come to the end. We are seeking to be *keepers of the flame*. And what does that require of us?

To maintain integrity *in our individual and corporate dealings inside and outside of our communities of faith.* We have seen that the altar of our lives must be built according to godly standards and upheld in both our immediate and distant relations with others. Those relationships, rooted in covenantal love, must be free of division, strife and pride so that we have a valid foundation upon which to base our worship.

To recapture a God-centered spirituality *that is based on raising up acceptable offerings from the work of our hands and the condition of our hearts.* An offering acceptable to God is one that remains on the altar at all times. Through all the trials that beset us, we must stay focused on maintaining the purity of our sacrifice before God.

Such an offering is not momentary or ritualistic, but is a call to covenant relationship walked out on a daily basis. Indeed, our sacrifice is our very life.

To foster within our lives that which pleases the Lord *and welcomes His presence in our midst.* We have learned that the Fire represents the presence of the One True and Living God, manifested and inhabiting the dwelling place of His people. The Holy One, blessed be He, is searching throughout the earth for a man, a woman, a people in whom He can show Himself faithful. The Fire cleanses, melts and burns away as it beckons us to enter its flame.

By receiving instruction and revelation in these three areas, we are now well-equipped to live our lives as worship unto our God.

The Heart of the Matter

So far, everything we have examined has been from our perspective. While we have sought to order our ways according to what is right, we have focused on what it means for us to be *keepers of the flame.* However, as you may have found out by this point in your walk with the Lord, you are not the center of the universe.

The question we must ask ourselves now is *why.*

Why are we building sound altars?

Why are we lifting acceptable sacrifices?

Why are we stoking the flame of His presence?

Is it to amuse ourselves? To entertain each other? To distract ourselves from the sorrow of life?

Worship is the absolute essence of our existence. But why must we live lives of worship? What is it that we're hoping for? Why is it that we keep this flame?

As you read through the exhortations surrounding the altar, the sacrifice and the fire; you may have asked yourself, *"Which of these is most important? Which one is the key to all the others? Which of these is God really looking for?"*

Each of us, by virtue of our personality, life experience and a host of other factors, will be drawn to one of these three elements; the altar, the sacrifice or the fire.

Those of us who are structurally-oriented will immediately focus on the necessity of proper order in things, the place of the altar. Whether it be in an entire city or within our own congregations, we feel that if we could just get unified and get our acts together, things would really start to happen and we would really see God's Kingdom released in greater measure.

THE HOLY ONE, BLESSED BE HE, IS SEARCHING THROUGHOUT THE EARTH FOR A MAN, A WOMAN, A PEOPLE IN WHOM HE CAN SHOW HIMSELF FAITHFUL.

Others of us concentrate on the sacrifice. For us, the issue is personal and corporate holiness and devotion to God. We reason that we are not seeing results in this age because our hearts are not right, and because we aren't willing to make those hard choices concerning our time and effort necessary to get the job done.

Finally, there are the fire people. We simply feel that the key to seeing massive change in the earth is taking off all controls and letting the Spirit come and, through massive demonstrations of power, have His way.

Most of us, though we may identify with one over the other, would say that all three elements are equally important. We would reason that God is concerned with receiving each of them.

While I believe that all of the functions we have considered up to this point are significant, I don't believe that, ultimately, God is looking for any one of them.

So, if God is not satisfied by the integrity of our relationships, the wholeness of our sacrifice or the blaze of our fire, what is it that God is looking for?

A Pleasing Aroma

Leviticus 1:9 declares, *"It is a burnt offering, an offering made by fire, an aroma pleasing to the LORD."*

Ultimately, what the Lord is looking for, what will move His heart and hand, is a fragrance. The Lord is looking for the fragrance that is released when all three of these components of the burnt offering are moving together in glorious unity.

This has been His desire from the very beginning.

The Aroma then

See the rough stones; which, though coarse with age and imperfect in and of themselves, have found a way to fit together to form a solid, sound structure. See the priest in his holy array as he lays down the slain animal. See the flicker of the undying flame, which has not been quenched; which has not gone out.

WORSHIP IS THE ABSOLUTE ESSENCE OF OUR EXISTENCE. BUT WHY MUST WE LIVE LIVES OF WORSHIP? WHAT IS IT THAT WE'RE HOPING FOR? WHY IS IT THAT WE KEEP THIS FLAME?

As the dead flesh meets the living flame, something happens. Immediately, smoke begins to rise up out of this place of convergence. Priest has met altar has met sacrifice has met fire—and all for this moment; this moment of release. The combination of these elements produces a reaction that would not be possible if any one were missing. Yet the reaction cannot be attributed solely to any one element alone. Suddenly, a fragrance is released that wafts heavenward, toward the nostrils of God.

The priest is to bring all of it and burn it on the altar; it is a burnt offering, an offering made by fire, an aroma pleasing to the LORD (Lev. 1:13).

The Aroma now: *thoughts for today*

As *the sweet-smelling fragrance* that rose to the Lord, the aroma was the element created from the synthesis of all the other elements. The **right relationships** we maintain are essential to the process of worship as they provide the foundation, the altar, of our lives. Without the **offerings** we present to the Lord through our service and whole-hearted devotion, there would be nothing to burn as a sacrifice. And without the **consuming fire** of God's presence marking our lives with worth and meaning, there would be no way of lifting our worship to heaven. When the altar, the sacrifice and the fire each fulfill their respective functions, something is created that brings pleasure to God.

THE THING GOD WANTS, THE ONE THING HE IS AFTER, IS THE SWEET AND BEAUTIFUL FRAGRANCE THAT RISES UP TO HIM WHEN THE ELEMENTS WITHIN OUR LIVES AND BETWEEN OUR LIVES AND OTHERS' UNITE IN HONOR AND HARMONY.

What God truly desires, what He considers true worship, is not contained in any one of these elements. The thing God wants, the one thing He is after, is the sweet and beautiful fragrance that rises up to Him when the elements within our lives and between our lives and others' unite in honor and harmony.

"But thanks be to God, who always leads us in triumphal procession in Christ and through us spreads everywhere the fragrance of the knowledge of him. For we are to God the aroma of Christ

among those who are being saved and those who are perishing"
(2 Cor. 2:14-15).

A Unified Perspective

Why is this fact so essential to our understanding of worship?

It is simply because each of us tends to value our worldview, our orientation, as more important and correct than anyone else's.

Those who focus on proper structure and organization (the "altar" people) can feel that those looking for the move of the Holy Spirit and powerful manifestations are flaky, marginal and out of order. Rather than focusing on allowing the Holy Spirit to penetrate their hearts in a life-changing way, they can spend their time strategizing and drawing up flow charts and job descriptions; waiting for everyone to see things their way.

THERE IS A DYNAMIC, A FORCE, AN AROMA THAT IS RELEASED WHEN EACH PART OF THE BODY PLAYS ITS ROLE, AND ALSO HONORS THE WORK AND CALLING OF THE OTHER, RECOGNIZING THE NEED FOR THE OTHERS INFLUENCE.

Those who focus on heart issues (the "sacrifice" people) can subtly feel that if everyone else were a little more broken and a little more yielded and committed that we would really be moving forward. An unseen self-righteousness can easily creep in, based on an individualistic mindset that waits for everyone else to get as spiritual and right with God as they are.

And those who focus on the power and manifestations of the Spirit (the "fire" people) can drift aimlessly from conference to conference, feeling that, really, the altar people are controlling and manipulative and if they would just get out of the way the Holy Spirit would really be able to break through. They are so "free" in the Spirit that they are not grounded in the level of real community, which authenticates our experiences.

No, if God really wanted one of these things over the other, if the Lord focused on one over the other, we would have a lopsided Kingdom.

A Beautiful Sight

God says that there is a dynamic, a force, an aroma that is released when each part of the body plays its role, and also honors the work and calling of the other, recognizing the need for the others influence. The intangible that is released is the Psalm 133 blessing that comes when we live God's Kingdom, God's way.

> *How good and pleasant it is*
> *when brothers live together in unity!*
> *It is like precious oil poured on the head,*
> *running down on the beard,*
> *running down on Aaron's beard,*
> *down upon the collar of his robes.*
> *It is as if the dew of Hermon*
> *were falling on Mount Zion.*
> *For there the* LORD *bestows his blessing,*
> *even life forevermore* (Ps. 133:2-3).

A Lovely Sound

In music, when two notes of a chord are played in absolute perfect pitch, there is a sound phenomena released in the atmosphere. A third tone appears; it is called the harmonic. Even though no instrument is playing it, and no one has touched that note, the sound is

THERE IS A CALL
GOING OUT IN
THE NATIONS.
THE LORD IS
LOOKING FOR THE
LEVITES OF GOD
TO ARISE.

audibly heard when the other notes are in absolute perfect pitch. This is what the fragrance of God is like in the midst of His people.

There is something REAL that comes, seemingly from out of nowhere, when God's people are offering an acceptable sacrifice to Him. It is real. It is there. And it is impossible to produce on demand. You can only create the right circumstances and conditions for it to appear. It simply happens when all else is in divine order.

An Aroma of Life

In these tumultuous days of human history, situations and conditions are arising on earth that are causing men's hearts to fail them for fear. At the same time, there is a call going out in the nations. The Lord is looking for the Levites of God to arise.

The Lord is looking for those priests after His heart and His purpose to come forth. He is looking for the dissatisfied, the hungry, the yearning, the perseverant, the desperate, the committed. God desires those who will prepare the way of the Lord.

An altar must be built. We must learn that doing the right thing in our interactions with others, counts. We must resolve to maintain firm foundations and tear down those structures that are not producing life.

A sacrifice must be raised. We must choose to believe, forgive and stand our ground as long as it takes until the fire comes and consumes our sacrifice.

The fire must remain. We must shift our mindsets to accommodate the burning, holy, consuming Spirit of the Lord. We cannot and must not continue to go through motions and feed systems that are not furthering His Kingdom. There IS a heavenly pattern that will release an earthly result.

Will you be a *keeper of the flame?*

Will you rearrange the altar of your life?

Will you bring the daily sacrifice of your all?

Will you stand in the fire that burns
and allow its searing flame to penetrate you to the core?

Will you wake up tomorrow and do it all over again?

Will you adopt a lifestyle given to the presence
and purpose of God being released through you
into everyone and everything you touch?

Will you sanctify all that is around you
because the aroma of God is on you?

Respond to the call of God. Hear His heart. What greater thing could we commit ourselves to?

The standard of what it means to belong to Him to walk with Him must be recaptured and raised in our time.

Become a part of the generation of the faithful called *keepers of the flame.*

KEEPERS OF THE FLAME: A COMMITMENT

Then the priest shall bring it [the offering] all
and burn it on the altar; it is a burnt sacrifice,
an offering made by fire, a sweet aroma to the LORD.

LEVITICUS 1:13 NKJV

Therefore, I urge you, brothers, in view of God's mercy,
to offer your bodies as living sacrifices,
holy and pleasing to God—
this is your spiritual act of worship.
Do not conform any longer to the pattern of this world,
but be transformed by the renewing of your mind.
Then you will be able to test and approve
what God's will is—his good, pleasing and perfect will.

ROMANS 12:1-2

As a *keeper of the flame,* I dedicate, consecrate and commit myself to:

Building the altar . . .
- Choosing a lifestyle of worship
- Abandoning myself totally to God
- Coming before Him wholeheartedly
- Paying the price of true worship
- Building an altar to the Lord in all my relationships

Offering the sacrifice . . .
- Placing my total being on the altar as my sacrifice
- Coming into God's presence to connect with Him
- Presenting the sacrifice of my hands, my time, my possessions, my work
- Deciding to obey; becoming a doer not just a hearer of the Word

Keeping the fire . . .
- Entering into and encountering the fire of God
- Being impassioned by a fiery love for God
- Desperately pursuing God
- Maintaining the fire as the ultimate priority in my life
- Seeking the fire of revelation
- Being consumed by the fire of purity and consecration
- Consecrating myself solely to Christ for His use

Releasing the fragrance . . .
- That the living God will be pleased with all that I am
- That the changes of holiness worked in me by the altar, sacrifice and fire might attract the world to Christ
- That all of my life would manifest God's love in me and through me to both the Church and the world

ADDITIONAL BOOKS
FROM
KAIROS PUBLISHING

Living in the Spirit of Revival - *Dr. Ron Burgio*
Are you ready to personally live in the Spirit of
Revival? Would you like your church not only to
experience revival, but also to maintain the Spirit of
revival for years after the newness and freshness wears
thin? Revival is for you and your church. Whether
you are a pastor, leader or believer hungry and
desperate for God, this book is for you. It's time to
experience the power and impact of revival in your
life today!
ISBN 0-9665831-3-2 $9.99

The Way of the Thorn - *David Trementozzi*
In brilliant fashion, reminiscent of *Pilgrims Progress*,
David Trementozzi squarely faces one of life's central
dilemmas—suffering. Drawing on the imagery of
Paul's thorn in the flesh, he masterfully weaves a tale
that not only brings understanding, but elicits hope.
PUBLISHED IN COOPERATION WITH EVERGREEN PRESS
ISBN 1-58169-097-5 $10.99

One People, Many Tribes - *Dr. Daniel C. Juster*
In this unique perspective on Church history,
Dr. Juster describes how the various restoration
movements in the history of the Church have served
to either hinder or help the Church come into greater
levels of New Testament truth.
ISBN 0-9665831-1-6 $9.99

Youth Can Minister - *Bruce & Lynn Latshaw*
Learn how Pastors Bruce and Lynn Latshaw have
successfully nurtured and released ON-FIRE
Christian youth into ministry. If you have a vision to
see qualified youth empowered and released to
impact their generation for Christ, this book will
encourage you and provide workable ways to
implement the vision!
ISBN 0-9674653-0-3 $9.99

Ten Commandments for Success - *Robert I. Winer, M.D.*
This book will shake loose false notions about the
most gifted Law Giver in the history of mankind and
reveal vital opportunities for greater success in every
aspect of your life.
ISBN 0-9655180-0-0 $4.99

Prices subject to change.

MAKING YOUR WORDS TIMELESS...

Will God's revelation to you this year be lost forever?

Each year, God gives you dynamic and lasting revelation through a series of messages or teachings that need to be preserved as a legacy for the coming generations of new people in your congregation and in other conference and ministry settings where you speak.

Your *kairos* moment of preaching or teaching may never again be preached by you from a pulpit, but it can become a lasting legacy for ongoing inspiration and revelation to others.

Provide your people each year with a book that they can reread over and over again and share with others. Leave a legacy. Develop an outstanding library of ministry resources for your people from what God has spoken to you.

Kairos Publishing can transform your notes, manuscripts and tapes or CDs into dynamic, cost-effective books for your ministry. Kairos Publishing can also market your books through the catalogues, magazines and events of Eagles' Wings.

Kairos Publishing is committed to producing material that will advance the Kingdom of God and call the Body of Christ to a place of intimacy. When God's timing and destiny meet, we believe a Spirit-breathed word comes forth, providing insight through hearts and souls that have been touched by His mighty hand.

KAIROS PUBLISHING is an entity of Eagles' Wings. Eagles' Wings is an international, relational network of believers who are committed to the unity of the Body of Christ, biblical spirituality through a lifestyle of worship and prayer, and the restoration of Israel.

For more information, please contact:

Kairos Publishing
PO Box 450
Clarence, NY 14031
Email: info@kairos.us
Website: www.kairos.us
Tel: 716.759.1058
Fax: 716.759.0731

EAGLES' WINGS

Eagles' Wings is an international relational network of believers, churches and ministries committed to the lifestyle of biblical spirituality through a lifestyle of worship and prayer, the unity of the Body of Christ, and the restoration of Israel.

Eagles' Wings is comprised of a full time staff of forty, under the leadership of an Advisory Board with Robert Stearns serving as Executive Director. Eagles' Wings has ministered in over thirty nations, and maintains active, ongoing ministry in Honduras and Israel.

PO BOX 450
CLARENCE, NY 14031

TEL: 716.759.1058

FAX: 716.759.0731

VISIT OUR WEBSITE:
WWW.EAGLESWINGS.TO

HA3B-A220

WORSHIP.

The River

LIVE WITH ROBERT STEARNS

The River Series of live worship was launched out of a place of waiting upon the Lord. Amazing sounds emerged as the Spirit had His way and moved in the lives of the worshippers.

"Musically powerful, lyrically poignant and spiritually alive, the one who engages this work will not remain unchanged."

— JOHN AUSMUS ON THE RIVER 5
WORSHIPMUSIC.COM